Option B Revolution

How Resilience Can Transform Your Life and Help You Overcome Life's Challenges

LEE M. HANSEN

the seller for any reparation, damage, or moneyrelated misfortune attributable to the data received, whether explicitly or indirectly. Those authors assert all copyrights which the seller does not retain. The statistics herein are solely for instructional purposes and are all. The details were reached without consent or acknowledgement of guarantee. The markings used shall be without permission, and without the approval or help of the proprietor of the label shall be published. All logos and trademarks in this book are for information purposes only and are held explicitly by individuals who are not affiliated with this document.

LIMITED LIABILITY DISCLAIMER

The author and publisher of this book, "Option B Revolution: Redefining Success in Life's Challenges," have made every effort to provide accurate and up-to-date information. However, they make no representations or warranties of any kind, express or implied, about the completeness, accuracy, reliability, suitability, or availability concerning the content contained within these pages. The information is provided for general informational purposes only.

The author and publisher shall not be liable for any loss, damage, or injury arising from the use of the information presented in this book. Readers are advised to verify and cross-reference the information provided herein with other sources and to seek professional advice if needed.

Any reliance you place on the information presented in this book is strictly at your own risk. The author and publisher disclaim any responsibility for any liability, loss, or risk incurred as a consequence, directly or indirectly, of the use and application of any of the contents of this book.

The mention of specific companies, organizations, products, or individuals in this book does not imply endorsement by the author or publisher. The views and opinions expressed in this book are those of the author and do not necessarily reflect the official policy or position of any other entity.

While efforts have been made to ensure that the information provided in this book is accurate and up-to-date, the author and publisher make no representations or warranties of any kind concerning the completeness, accuracy, reliability, or suitability of the information for any purpose.

By reading this book, you agree that the author and publisher shall not be responsible or liable for any loss, injury, claim, liability, or damage of any kind resulting from or related to the use of the information presented in this book.

TABLE OF CONTENTS

Introduction: Embracing Life's Challenges and the Option B Revolution

The concept of the Option B Revolution as a paradigm shift in facing life's challenges

In the realm of navigating life's tumultuous journey, the Option B Revolution emerges as a compelling paradigm shift, challenging conventional notions of success and resilience. This revolution is not just a concept; it's a transformative approach to embracing the unexpected, the setbacks, and the trials that define our existence. It invites individuals to reevaluate their perspectives and redefine success, fostering a mindset that thrives amid adversity.

At its core, the Option B Revolution encourages a departure from the rigid frameworks that often confine our understanding of achievement. Instead of adhering strictly to predefined paths, it propels us to explore the untapped potential within adversity, transforming challenges into catalysts for personal and societal growth. This shift in mindset transcends the binary notion of success and failure, introducing a nuanced understanding that acknowledges the richness of experience embedded in life's struggles.

The foundation of this revolutionary concept lies in recognizing that life is inherently unpredictable, marked by unforeseen twists and turns. Rather than succumbing to the despair that accompanies setbacks, the Option B Revolution prompts individuals to embrace the inherent flexibility of their life narratives. It advocates for an active and intentional engagement with adversity, urging people to view challenges not as roadblocks but as opportunities for profound self-discovery.

In a world fixated on celebrating only the triumphant moments, the Option B Revolution redefines success by appreciating the resilience demonstrated in the face of adversity. It propels us beyond the confines of societal expectations, urging a shift from external validation to an internal compass that guides us through life's storms. This new paradigm encourages a deeper exploration of personal values and convictions, fostering a sense of purpose that transcends the ephemeral nature of conventional success.

Central to the Option B Revolution is the idea that resilience is not a passive state but an active, ongoing process. It challenges individuals to cultivate resilience as a skill, honing the ability to adapt, learn, and grow in the face of adversity. This perspective empowers individuals to view setbacks not as insurmountable obstacles but as opportunities for skill development and personal evolution.

Furthermore, the Option B Revolution dismantles the myth of a linear life journey, emphasizing that setbacks are not detours but integral parts of the narrative. By reframing the narrative, individuals can find meaning and purpose even in the most challenging chapters of their lives. This revolution encourages a holistic view of success—one that encompasses not only professional achievements but also personal growth, relationships, and the pursuit of genuine happiness.

As individuals embrace the Option B Revolution, they become architects of their narratives, weaving resilience into the fabric of their life stories. It prompts a reevaluation of societal benchmarks, encouraging a more inclusive definition of success that accommodates diverse paths and experiences. In doing so, it challenges the prevailing narrative that success is a one-size-fits-all concept and promotes a more compassionate and understanding society.

The necessity of redefining success in the face of adversity

In the crucible of life's challenges, the imperative to redefine success becomes increasingly apparent, transcending conventional parameters and beckoning individuals to introspect on the true essence of achievement. Adversity, with its unpredictable nature, demands a departure from the stereotypical markers of success, urging a more nuanced and resilient perspective.

At the heart of the necessity to redefine success lies the acknowledgment that adversity is an intrinsic part of the human experience. Life's journey is fraught with unexpected twists, setbacks, and moments of profound difficulty. Conventional definitions of success often fail to account for these inevitable challenges, creating a narrow and unrealistic framework that overlooks the richness found in navigating adversity.

In the face of adversity, the conventional view of success as a linear trajectory towards predetermined goals begins to unravel. The rigidity of traditional success metrics proves inadequate in capturing the complexities of human experience, leaving individuals ill-equipped to navigate the storms that life invariably brings. It is in these moments of upheaval that the imperative to redefine success emerges as a beacon of resilience, guiding individuals through the uncharted waters of their personal and professional lives.

Redefining success in the context of adversity involves a fundamental shift from external validation to an internal compass. The external markers of success—such as wealth, status, or recognition—may falter in the face of life's challenges. Embracing a more intrinsic and values-driven definition of success allows individuals to cultivate a resilient mindset that thrives irrespective of external circumstances. This recalibration invites individuals to consider success not merely as the attainment of goals but as a dynamic and evolving process of growth, learning, and adaptation.

Moreover, redefining success in the face of adversity is a rejection of the societal pressure to conform to a predetermined narrative. The traditional narrative often dictates that success follows a linear path, free of detours or obstacles. However, such a perspective discounts the inherent value embedded in setbacks and challenges. By redefining success, individuals can transform adversity from a stumbling block into a stepping stone, viewing each setback as an opportunity for introspection, learning, and personal evolution.

A crucial aspect of this redefinition is the integration of resilience into the very fabric of success. Resilience, as an active and intentional response to adversity, becomes a cornerstone of this new paradigm. Instead of viewing setbacks as failures, individuals can embrace them as integral components of their success stories, each trial contributing to the development of resilience as a skill. In this way, redefining success aligns closely with the cultivation of a mindset that views challenges not as insurmountable barriers but as avenues for self-discovery and growth.

Furthermore, the necessity to redefine success in the face of adversity extends beyond individual well-being to societal progress. A society that rigidly adheres to conventional success metrics may inadvertently marginalize those who do not fit the predefined mold. Redefining success encourages a more inclusive and compassionate society, one that recognizes and celebrates diverse paths, experiences, and definitions of achievement. In this way, the collective reevaluation of success becomes a catalyst for broader social transformation, fostering empathy, understanding, and a shared commitment to resilience.

Resilience, growth, and transformation through life's difficulties

As the curtains rise on the pages of "Option B Revolution: Redefining Success in Life's Challenges," the overture resounds with a resounding theme—life's difficulties are not impediments but catalysts for profound resilience, growth, and transformation. In this narrative, adversity is not a dark adversary to be feared, but rather a crucible that forges the indomitable spirit of the human experience.

The tone of this book is one of unwavering optimism, grounded in the belief that within the ebb and flow of life's challenges lies an untapped reservoir of strength and potential. It invites readers to embark on a journey, not of avoidance or escape from difficulties, but of deliberate engagement—a dance with adversity that transforms stumbling blocks into stepping stones.

At the heart of this symphony is the concept of resilience—a dynamic force that propels individuals forward in the face of life's adversities. Resilience, in the context of this book, is not a passive state but an active and intentional response to challenges. It is the art of bending without breaking, of drawing strength from setbacks, and of navigating the intricate twists of life with a steadfast spirit. Each chapter resonates with stories of individuals who, faced with seemingly insurmountable odds, discovered reservoirs of resilience within themselves, illuminating the transformative power of navigating challenges with a resilient mindset.

Growth emerges as a central theme interwoven into the fabric of this narrative. The book contends that growth is not confined to moments of triumph but is intricately linked to the crucible of adversity. It challenges the notion that growth is a linear progression and posits that the most profound transformations often arise from the crucible of life's difficulties. Through anecdotes, research, and exploration, readers are encouraged to embrace the notion that setbacks are not interruptions to personal development but integral components of a continuous and enriching journey towards self-discovery.

Transformation, the crescendo of this symphony, is portrayed as the natural outcome of resilience and growth. It is the metamorphosis that occurs when individuals confront, adapt, and transcend challenges. The book celebrates stories of transformation—individuals who, in the face of adversity, emerged not just stronger but fundamentally changed for the better. It underscores that transformation is not an endpoint but a continual process, emphasizing that the journey itself, with all its ups and downs, is the true canvas of transformation.

The narrative unfolds with a recognition that life's difficulties are diverse, ranging from personal crises to professional challenges, from unforeseen twists of fate to societal upheavals. The book casts a wide net, drawing inspiration from a myriad of experiences and perspectives. It invites readers to embrace the universality of challenges while acknowledging the uniqueness of individual journeys.

Intertwined with stories of resilience, growth, and transformation are practical insights and actionable strategies. The book is not just a collection of narratives but a guide—an empowering toolkit that equips readers with the tools to cultivate resilience, navigate growth, and initiate transformative change in their own lives.

Moreover, the tone is one of inclusivity, recognizing that the journey through life's difficulties is a shared human experience. It celebrates diversity in adversity, acknowledging that the human spirit is a mosaic shaped by a myriad of backgrounds, experiences, and perspectives. In doing so, the book fosters a sense of community, inviting readers to see themselves not as solitary travelers but as part of a collective narrative of resilience and triumph.

Chapter 1: Redefining Success: Beyond Conventional Measures

Conventional notions of success and their limitations

In the vast landscape of human aspirations, conventional notions of success have long held sway, offering a roadmap that promises fulfillment, recognition, and contentment.

However, as we navigate the complex terrain of personal and professional life, it becomes imperative to scrutinize and unravel these conventional ideas, recognizing both their merits and, perhaps more importantly, their limitations.

The conventional paradigm of success often manifests as a linear trajectory, marked by predefined milestones such as academic achievements, career advancements, and material acquisitions. This traditional framework, while providing a sense of direction, can inadvertently confine individuals within rigid expectations, stifling creativity, and personal exploration. The very nature of this linear model implies a predetermined endpoint, fostering a mindset that places undue emphasis on outcomes rather than the journey itself.

Furthermore, conventional notions of success are frequently tied to external validations— measures such as wealth, social status, and public recognition. This externalized definition can create a precarious foundation, as it relies on factors beyond one's control. The limitations of this approach become glaringly apparent when faced with life's uncertainties and setbacks, as it fails to account for the inherent ebb and flow of the human experience.

Another limitation lies in the narrow definition of success that often neglects the multifaceted nature of the human journey. The traditional narrative tends to prioritize professional accomplishments at the expense of personal growth, relationships, and overall well-being. This narrow focus can lead individuals to overlook the richness found in the tapestry of life, fostering a myopic perspective that neglects the holistic nature of success.

Moreover, the conventional paradigm tends to perpetuate a comparative mindset—a relentless pursuit of benchmarks set by societal norms or peer achievements. The constant comparison to external standards can breed discontent and undermine one's sense of self-worth. The emphasis on outperforming others, rather than pursuing personal fulfillment, can create an insatiable thirst for validation, perpetuating a cycle of stress and unfulfillment.

In dissecting these limitations, it is essential to recognize the dynamic nature of success and its intrinsic connection to personal values and aspirations. Success, when viewed through a broader lens, encompasses not only external achievements but also internal satisfaction, personal growth, and meaningful connections. This expanded perspective invites individuals to redefine success on their terms, aligning their goals with their values and embracing a more authentic and fulfilling path.

The limitations of conventional success are further underscored by its static nature, often failing to accommodate the evolving nature of personal and societal values. As society progresses and paradigms shift, what once constituted success may lose relevance. Adherence to outdated benchmarks can result in a disconnection from one's authentic self and a sense of unfulfillment.

In the face of these limitations, the need for a paradigm shift becomes evident. The exploration of alternative definitions of success that transcend the constraints of the conventional model is essential. Embracing a more fluid, adaptable, and personalized understanding of success allows individuals to navigate the complexities of life with resilience and authenticity.

The journey to redefine success involves a process of introspection, self-discovery, and a conscious alignment of personal values with life goals. It encourages individuals to break free from the shackles of comparison, embrace the uniqueness of their path, and find fulfillment in the pursuit of purpose rather than external validation.

The impact of societal expectations on individual well-being

In the intricate dance between individual aspirations and societal expectations, the profound influence of the latter on personal well-being cannot be overstated. Societal expectations, a complex web of norms, values, and benchmarks, weave their way into the fabric of our lives, shaping perceptions of success, happiness, and fulfillment. As we navigate this labyrinth, it becomes crucial to unravel the impact of societal expectations and explore avenues for preserving and enhancing individual well-being.

Societal expectations often act as silent architects, constructing a blueprint that outlines the "ideal" life path. From academic achievements to career milestones, relationships to personal milestones, these expectations create a standard against which individuals measure their own progress. While aspirations can provide motivation, the rigid adherence to societal benchmarks can morph into a double-edged sword, fostering a sense of inadequacy when one's journey deviates from the prescribed norm.

One of the pervasive impacts of societal expectations is the pressure to conform to predefined roles and trajectories. Individuals may find themselves navigating a predetermined script, adhering to societal norms even if it means sacrificing personal authenticity and genuine happiness. This pressure to conform can lead to a sense of alienation, as individuals grapple with the conflict between societal expectations and their intrinsic values and desires.

Moreover, the pursuit of external validation, often fueled by societal expectations, becomes a pivotal factor in individual well-being. The constant need for approval, whether in the form of social recognition, professional success, or material possessions, can create a perpetual cycle of seeking external validation for one's worth. This externalized validation, however, is inherently fleeting and can leave individuals feeling hollow and unfulfilled when it becomes the primary measure of their well-being.

The impact of societal expectations on mental health is profound. The relentless pursuit of societal benchmarks can contribute to stress, anxiety, and feelings of inadequacy. The fear of falling short of societal ideals can manifest as imposter syndrome, where individuals doubt their abilities and feel undeserving of their accomplishments. The toll on mental health is exacerbated by the societal stigma surrounding vulnerability and the reluctance to openly discuss the challenges of navigating these expectations.

Relationships, a cornerstone of well-being, are not immune to the influence of societal expectations. Expectations about the "ideal" partner, family dynamics, and life milestones can exert pressure on individuals to conform to societal norms in their personal lives. This can lead to a compromise of individual values and a sense of dissatisfaction in relationships that don't align with societal expectations.

However, it is essential to recognize the nuanced interplay between societal expectations and cultural context. Cultural expectations shape societal norms, and the impact on individual well-being can vary across different cultural landscapes. While some cultural expectations may provide a sense of belonging and identity, others may impose constraints that limit personal freedom and hinder well-being.

In confronting the impact of societal expectations, individuals have the agency to redefine success on their terms. This involves a process of self-discovery, introspection, and a deliberate alignment of personal values with societal norms. It requires breaking free from the constraints of comparison and embracing the uniqueness of one's journey, recognizing that well-being is a subjective experience that transcends external validation.

The collective responsibility to challenge and reshape societal expectations also comes to the forefront. It involves fostering open dialogues about the unrealistic standards set by society and promoting inclusivity that accommodates diverse paths and definitions of success. Societal change begins with individual empowerment, as individuals collectively question, challenge, and reshape the narratives that influence well-being.

Introduce the idea of expanding the definition of success to encompass personal growth and resilience

In a world often fixated on conventional metrics of success—ranging from financial achievements to professional milestones—it becomes imperative to broaden our understanding of what it means to thrive in the complex tapestry of life. The concept of success, when expanded beyond traditional boundaries, invites us to consider personal growth and resilience as paramount factors in the pursuit of a fulfilled and meaningful life.

At its essence, expanding the definition of success is an invitation to embark on a journey of holistic self-discovery and development. Rather than confining success to external markers or societal benchmarks, this paradigm shift encourages individuals to embrace a more profound and nuanced perspective. Success is not merely the attainment of predetermined goals but a dynamic, ongoing process that intertwines with personal growth—a continuous evolution that transcends the boundaries of traditional success metrics.

Personal growth emerges as a cornerstone in this expanded definition of success. It entails a deliberate and introspective journey toward self-improvement, learning, and the cultivation of one's full potential. Embracing personal growth as a measure of success shifts the focus from external validations to an internal compass, guiding individuals toward a deeper understanding of themselves and their aspirations. It is a recognition that success is not a stagnant endpoint but a continuous unfolding of one's capabilities and capacities.

Resilience, as a complementary pillar, plays a pivotal role in reshaping the contours of success. The expanded definition acknowledges that setbacks and challenges are inherent to the human experience. Rather than viewing obstacles as insurmountable roadblocks, resilience empowers individuals to navigate through adversity with courage, adaptability, and an unwavering determination to emerge stronger on the other side. Success, in this paradigm, is not immune to challenges but is intimately entwined with the ability to weather storms and extract valuable lessons from life's difficulties.

The conventional narrative often separates success from the intricate dance with failure and setbacks. However, expanding the definition of success dismantles this dichotomy, portraying setbacks not as failures but as integral components of a transformative journey. Resilience becomes a narrative thread, weaving through the fabric of success stories, emphasizing that the ability to bounce back from challenges is as significant as the achievements themselves.

Moreover, this paradigm shift encourages individuals to view success through a lens that transcends the individual realm and extends to the collective well-being of society. Success is not solely an individual pursuit but a collective journey where personal growth and resilience contribute to a thriving community. A society that values and fosters the growth and resilience of its members creates a fertile ground for innovation, empathy, and a shared commitment to overcoming challenges.

In practical terms, expanding the definition of success involves a conscious effort to set goals that align with personal values and contribute to holistic well-being. It invites individuals to reflect on the multifaceted aspects of their lives—career, relationships, personal development, and mental well-being—and integrate these elements into their understanding of success. The pursuit of success becomes a harmonious symphony, with personal growth and resilience as integral notes that complement and enrich the entire composition.

The stories of individuals who have embraced this expanded definition of success serve as beacons of inspiration. These narratives depict individuals who, despite facing setbacks, found profound meaning in the process of personal growth and resilience. Their journeys underscore that success, when viewed through the prism of growth and resilience, becomes a deeply fulfilling and transformative experience.

Chapter 2: The Psychology of Resilience: Navigating Life's Unforeseen Turns

Psychological aspects of resilience in the face of challenges

In the intricate tapestry of the human experience, resilience emerges as the psychological linchpin that determines not only how we navigate challenges but also how we grow and thrive in their wake. The exploration of resilience delves into the complex interplay of thoughts, emotions, and coping mechanisms that constitute the mind's fortress in the face of adversity. Understanding the psychological aspects of resilience unravels the mysteries of human endurance, providing insights into the profound capacities of the mind to adapt, learn, and triumph over life's difficulties.

At its core, resilience is not a fixed trait but a dynamic process shaped by various psychological factors. The cognitive dimensions of resilience encompass the way individuals perceive and interpret adversity. The resilient mind exhibits a cognitive flexibility that allows for adaptive thinking, enabling individuals to reframe challenges as opportunities for growth rather than insurmountable obstacles. This cognitive reframing is not a mere positive thinking exercise but a profound shift in perspective that empowers individuals to extract meaning from adversity and envision a path forward.

Emotional resilience, a closely entwined aspect, involves the regulation and expression of emotions in response to challenges. The psychologically resilient individual does not suppress or deny emotions but navigates them with a sense of self-awareness and self-regulation. Emotional intelligence becomes a guiding force, enabling individuals to harness the energy of emotions, whether fear, sadness, or anger, as a source of motivation and insight rather than succumbing to their destructive potential.

Moreover, the concept of learned helplessness—a psychological state where individuals perceive no control over their circumstances—stands in stark contrast to the resilient mindset. Resilient individuals perceive a sense of agency even in the face of adversity, believing in their capacity to influence outcomes through their actions. This belief in one's efficacy becomes a psychological anchor, preventing the descent into a state of helplessness and fostering a proactive engagement with challenges.

The psychological dimensions of resilience also encompass the cultivation of a growth mindset. A growth mindset, as conceptualized by psychologist Carol Dweck, involves the belief that abilities and intelligence can be developed through dedication and hard work. Resilient individuals tend to embrace challenges as opportunities to learn and improve, viewing setbacks not as reflections of their inherent capabilities but as stepping stones toward mastery. This mindset shift contributes significantly to the ability to bounce back from adversity with newfound wisdom and skills.

Furthermore, the role of self-efficacy, a concept introduced by psychologist Albert Bandura, is integral to understanding the psychological foundation of resilience. Self-efficacy refers to an individual's belief in their ability to execute specific actions to achieve desired outcomes. High self-efficacy acts as a psychological catalyst, empowering individuals to approach challenges with confidence, persistence, and a belief that they possess the skills necessary to overcome obstacles.

The social dimension of resilience is another psychological aspect that cannot be overlooked. Social support, whether from family, friends, or communities, plays a crucial role in bolstering psychological resilience. The presence of a supportive network provides individuals with a psychological safety net, offering emotional validation, practical assistance, and a sense of belonging that enhances the capacity to endure and rebound from adversity.

Moreover, the psychological aspect of post-traumatic growth sheds light on the transformative potential of resilience. While adversity can induce profound stress and upheaval, resilient individuals often experience post-traumatic growth—an emergence from adversity with an enhanced sense of personal strength, a deeper appreciation for life, and a reevaluation of priorities and values.

Components of resilience and their application in overcoming adversity

In the crucible of life's challenges, resilience stands as a beacon of strength, guiding individuals through the tumultuous waters of adversity. The components of resilience, multifaceted and interconnected, form a dynamic framework that empowers individuals not only to endure adversity but to emerge from it with newfound strength and wisdom. This exploration delves into the essential components of resilience and their transformative application in overcoming life's most formidable challenges.

1. **Cognitive Flexibility:** At the heart of resilience lies cognitive flexibility—a mental agility that allows individuals to adapt their thinking in response to adversity. This component involves the ability to reframe challenges, viewing setbacks not as insurmountable obstacles but as opportunities for growth. Cognitive flexibility enables individuals to navigate adversity with a mindset that seeks solutions, fosters learning, and finds meaning in the face of difficulties.

2. **Emotional Regulation:** Resilience is intimately tied to emotional regulation—the capacity to navigate and manage emotions effectively. Rather than suppressing or succumbing to negative emotions, resilient individuals harness them as valuable signals. Emotional regulation involves self-awareness, allowing individuals to recognize and understand their emotions, and self-regulation, enabling them to respond to challenges with a balanced emotional state.

3. **Sense of Purpose and Meaning:** Resilience draws strength from a deep sense of purpose and meaning. Individuals with a clear understanding of their values and a sense of purpose that extends beyond immediate circumstances often exhibit heightened resilience. This component provides a guiding light in the darkest moments, anchoring individuals to a broader narrative that transcends the challenges at hand.

4. **Learned Optimism:** The concept of learned optimism, pioneered by psychologist Martin Seligman, underscores the importance of cultivating a positive outlook. Resilient individuals

tend to exhibit learned optimism, viewing setbacks as temporary and specific rather than permanent and pervasive. This cognitive reframing enhances one's ability to bounce back from adversity, fostering a belief in the malleability of circumstances.

5. **Adaptive Coping Strategies:** Resilience involves the intentional deployment of adaptive coping strategies—resourceful approaches that individuals employ to navigate challenges. These strategies may include problem-solving, seeking social support, maintaining a healthy lifestyle, and fostering a growth mindset. The application of adaptive coping mechanisms enables individuals to confront adversity with a proactive and empowered stance.

6. **Social Support Networks:** The significance of social support in resilience cannot be overstated. Building and maintaining robust social support networks provide a psychological safety net during challenging times. Whether through family, friends, or community, the presence of a supportive network offers emotional validation, practical assistance, and a sense of belonging that

enhances an individual's resilience in the face of adversity.

7. **Self-Efficacy:** Resilience is intricately linked to self-efficacy—the belief in one's ability to execute actions that lead to desired outcomes. High self-efficacy empowers individuals to approach challenges with confidence, persistence, and a belief in their capacity to influence outcomes. This psychological component forms a cornerstone in the transformative application of resilience, shaping the way individuals perceive and respond to adversity.

8. **Post-Traumatic Growth:** Resilience transcends mere recovery; it encompasses the potential for post-traumatic growth. Individuals who cultivate resilience often experience transformative growth in the aftermath of adversity. This growth involves an enhanced sense of personal strength, a deeper appreciation for life, the reevaluation of priorities, and a profound shift in values.

The transformative application of these resilience components becomes evident in the stories of individuals who have navigated and overcome profound challenges. The ability to adapt cognitively, regulate emotions, find purpose, cultivate optimism, deploy adaptive coping strategies, nurture social support, bolster self-efficacy, and experience post-traumatic growth collectively forms a comprehensive toolkit for confronting and transcending adversity.

In real-world scenarios, resilience is not a passive trait but an active engagement with life's difficulties. It is a skill that can be cultivated and honed through intentional practices, self-reflection, and a commitment to continuous growth. By understanding and applying these components of resilience, individuals can forge a path through adversity that not only withstands the trials of the moment but emerges stronger, wiser, and more resilient on the other side. Resilience, in its transformative application, becomes a guiding force that shapes not only how individuals confront challenges but also how they evolve and thrive in the aftermath of adversity.

Developing a resilient mindset for navigating life's unexpected twists

Life's journey, marked by unpredictable twists and turns, demands a mindset of resilience—an unwavering spirit capable of navigating the unexpected with grace and determination. Developing a resilient mindset is not merely a response to adversity but an intentional and transformative approach to life. This exploration provides insights into the art of cultivating a resilient mindset, offering a roadmap for individuals to not only endure life's surprises but to flourish in their wake.

1. **Embrace Change as a Constant:** A resilient mindset begins with a fundamental acceptance of change as an inherent part of life. Rather than resisting or fearing the unknown, individuals with a resilient mindset view change as a constant force, recognizing that adaptation is key to thriving in an ever-evolving world. Embracing change fosters a mindset that is agile, open, and capable of finding opportunity within uncertainty.

2. **Develop Cognitive Flexibility:** Cultivating a resilient mindset involves developing cognitive flexibility—the ability to adapt one's thinking in response to unexpected situations. Instead of being bound by rigid expectations or preconceived notions, individuals with cognitive flexibility are adept at reframing challenges, finding alternative perspectives, and leveraging creative problem-solving skills. This adaptive thinking is a cornerstone of resilience.

3. **Foster a Growth Mindset:** At the core of a resilient mindset is a growth-oriented perspective. Embracing a growth mindset, as articulated by psychologist Carol Dweck, involves seeing challenges as opportunities for learning and growth. Individuals with a growth mindset perceive setbacks not as failures but as stepping stones toward personal and professional development, fostering a resilient approach to life's twists.

4. **Build Emotional Intelligence:** Emotional intelligence is a crucial element in developing resilience. A resilient mindset involves understanding and regulating emotions effectively. Rather than being overwhelmed by negative emotions, individuals with emotional intelligence navigate them with self-awareness, allowing for a balanced response to life's unexpected challenges. This emotional regulation is instrumental in maintaining composure and making sound decisions in the face of uncertainty.

5. **Cultivate Adaptability:** Resilience thrives in an environment of adaptability. Developing a resilient mindset involves cultivating adaptability—a willingness to adjust plans, pivot when necessary, and

embrace new opportunities that arise unexpectedly. An adaptable mindset enables individuals to flow with the unpredictable currents of life rather than resisting them, fostering a sense of control amid uncertainty.

6. **Find Meaning in Adversity:** A resilient mindset involves seeking meaning in the midst of adversity. Individuals who navigate life's unexpected twists with resilience often find purpose and significance in their experiences. This sense of meaning becomes a guiding force, providing a anchor in turbulent times and empowering individuals to endure challenges with a greater sense of purpose.

7. **Cultivate Self-Compassion:** Resilience requires a foundation of self-compassion—a gentle and understanding approach toward oneself, especially in times of difficulty. Rather than succumbing to self-criticism, individuals with a resilient mindset practice self-compassion, recognizing that facing unexpected challenges is a universal aspect of the human experience. This self-compassion becomes a source of inner strength during tumultuous times.

8. **Build a Supportive Network:** A resilient mindset is nurtured within the context of a supportive social network. Developing connections with others who share similar values and a resilient outlook provides a valuable source of encouragement and understanding. In times of unexpected challenges, a supportive network becomes a crucial resource, offering both emotional and practical assistance.

9. **Cultivate a Sense of Humor:** Humor is a powerful tool in developing a resilient mindset. The ability to find humor in life's unexpected twists can serve as a coping mechanism, alleviating stress and providing a perspective that transcends momentary difficulties. A lighthearted approach to challenges fosters resilience by preventing situations from becoming overwhelming.

10. **Practice Mindfulness:** Mindfulness, the practice of being fully present and aware in the moment, is integral to developing a resilient mindset. This intentional focus on the present moment allows individuals to navigate challenges with clarity and composure. Mindfulness practices, such as meditation and deep-breathing

exercises, provide tools for managing
stress and enhancing resilience.

Chapter 3: Option B Mindset: Embracing Alternatives and Possibilities

Option B Mindset As A Shift Towards Embracing Alternatives And Possibilities

In the intricate dance of life, unforeseen challenges and unexpected twists often force us to confront the limitations of our plans and expectations. It is within this unpredictable terrain that the Option B mindset emerges as a transformative and empowering perspective. Unlike the rigidity of a single, predetermined path, the Option B mindset invites individuals to consider alternatives and possibilities when faced with setbacks. It represents a paradigm shift—a departure from the constraints of a singular narrative towards a mindset that not only embraces alternatives but recognizes the inherent richness found in the exploration of diverse paths.

At its core, the Option B mindset acknowledges the reality that life rarely unfolds according to a linear script. Instead of viewing detours, setbacks, or unexpected changes as roadblocks, this mindset encourages individuals to perceive them as opportunities for exploration and growth. It embodies the spirit of resilience, adaptability, and a refusal to be confined by the limitations of adversity. The metaphorical "Option B" becomes a gateway to a myriad of possibilities, urging individuals to reimagine their journey and find fulfillment in unexpected places.

This mindset shift involves reframing adversity not as a dead-end but as a pivot point—a juncture where the narrative takes an unexpected turn. In doing so, it fosters a sense of agency, empowering individuals to make conscious choices in response to challenges. The Option B mindset is about recognizing that, in the face of adversity, individuals possess the capacity to redefine their goals, aspirations, and the very essence of success itself.

Central to the Option B mindset is the notion of embracing alternatives. It encourages individuals to let go of the notion that there is only one correct path or a singular definition of success. Instead, it champions the idea that, in the face of unexpected challenges, alternatives can lead to equally, if not more, fulfilling outcomes. This mindset is an acknowledgment that life's tapestry is woven with diverse threads, each offering its own unique texture and beauty.

Possibilities, within the context of the Option B mindset, are not confined by preconceived notions or societal expectations. They extend beyond the limitations of conventional success, inviting individuals to explore avenues that align with their evolving values, aspirations, and personal growth. The very act of considering alternatives opens a realm of creativity, innovation, and the discovery of untapped potentials that may have remained dormant in the absence of adversity.

Moreover, the Option B mindset challenges the dichotomy of success and failure. Instead of viewing setbacks as a mark of failure, it sees them as integral to the journey of growth and self-discovery. This perspective shift liberates individuals from the burden of perfectionism, allowing them to approach challenges with a sense of curiosity, resilience, and the understanding that setbacks are not the end but a continuation of the journey.

In practical terms, embracing the Option B mindset involves a commitment to continuous learning and adaptation. It requires individuals to be open to new experiences, to cultivate a mindset of curiosity, and to embrace the uncertainties that come with exploring alternatives. This mindset is not about denying the challenges or difficulties that may arise; rather, it is about navigating them with a spirit of flexibility, creativity, and a belief in one's ability to adapt and thrive.

The stories of those who have embodied the Option B mindset resonate as narratives of resilience, triumph, and unexpected joy. These individuals did not succumb to the limitations of setbacks; instead, they embraced alternatives, discovered new possibilities, and redefined success on their terms. Their journeys serve as inspiring testaments to the transformative power of embracing the unexpected and finding strength in the face of adversity.

The power of reframing challenges as opportunities for growth

Embracing the power of reframing challenges as opportunities for growth is a transformative shift in perspective that holds the potential to reshape the narrative of our lives. At its core, reframing is a cognitive skill that involves altering the way we perceive and interpret challenges. Rather than viewing setbacks as insurmountable obstacles, reframing invites us to see them as fertile ground for personal and intellectual development. This shift in mindset transcends mere positivity; it is a conscious choice to extract meaning and learning from adversity, unlocking a profound source of resilience and inner strength.

When challenges arise, the default response for many individuals is often one of resistance or avoidance. The discomfort and uncertainty that accompany adversity can be daunting, leading to a desire to sidestep or mitigate the impact of the challenge. However, the power of reframing lies in the recognition that challenges, far from being unwelcome intruders, can serve as catalysts for personal and professional advancement. It is a deliberate effort to view setbacks not as roadblocks but as pivotal moments that can propel us forward on the path of growth.

One of the key aspects of reframing challenges as opportunities for growth is the cultivation of a growth mindset. This concept, popularized by psychologist Carol Dweck, involves the belief that abilities and intelligence can be developed through dedication and effort. Individuals with a growth mindset see challenges as a natural part of the learning process, understanding that the journey itself, with its highs and lows, contributes to their development. By embracing a growth mindset, challenges cease to be threats and become stepping stones toward mastery and self-discovery.

Moreover, reframing challenges invites a reassessment of the concept of failure. Instead of viewing setbacks as a reflection of personal inadequacy or as the endpoint of a journey, individuals who embrace reframing see them as opportunities to learn, adapt, and recalibrate their approach. Failures are reframed as feedback, providing valuable insights into areas that require attention, adjustment, or a different perspective. This perspective on failure diminishes its negative connotations, transforming it into a dynamic force that propels individuals forward.

The power of reframing also lies in its ability to foster resilience in the face of adversity. Resilience is not about avoiding challenges but about bouncing back from them with newfound strength and insight. When challenges are reframed as opportunities for growth, individuals are more likely to approach them with a sense of curiosity and a belief in their ability to navigate difficulties. The process of reframing instills a sense of agency, empowering individuals to respond to challenges with adaptability and a constructive mindset.

Furthermore, reframing challenges as opportunities for growth promotes a mindset of abundance rather than scarcity. In a scarcity mindset, challenges are seen as threats that deplete resources and opportunities. However, reframing shifts this perspective by recognizing that challenges bring with them the abundance of possibilities for learning, innovation, and personal development. The mindset of abundance allows individuals to approach challenges with optimism, curiosity, and a willingness to explore new avenues.

Practically applying the power of reframing involves developing self-awareness and adopting intentional cognitive strategies. It requires a conscious effort to question automatic negative thoughts and replace them with more constructive interpretations. This process may involve seeking alternative viewpoints, considering the long-term benefits of the challenge, or identifying potential areas of personal growth that can emerge from the experience.

Provide practical strategies for adopting an Option B perspective in various aspects of life
Adopting an Option B perspective in various aspects of life is a dynamic and intentional approach that involves embracing resilience, exploring alternatives, and finding strength in the face of unexpected challenges. This mindset shift extends beyond mere theory; it necessitates practical strategies that individuals can integrate into different facets of their lives. From personal relationships to professional pursuits, implementing an Option B perspective involves a deliberate and transformative application of

strategies that foster adaptability, growth, and a profound sense of empowerment.

1. **Cultivate a Growth Mindset:** At the core of the Option B perspective is the cultivation of a growth mindset. Embracing challenges as opportunities for learning and development is foundational to this mindset. Individuals can actively foster a growth mindset by reframing setbacks as a natural part of the learning process, recognizing that abilities can be developed through dedication and effort. By adopting this perspective, challenges become not only manageable but essential components of personal and professional growth.

2. **Practice Resilience-Building Activities:** Resilience is a muscle that can be strengthened through intentional practices. Engaging in resilience-building activities, such as mindfulness meditation, yoga, or journaling, provides individuals with tools to navigate challenges with composure and adaptability. These activities enhance self-awareness, emotional regulation, and the capacity to bounce back from setbacks, aligning perfectly with the Option B perspective.

3. **Set Realistic and Flexible Goals:** In adopting an Option B perspective, it is crucial to set realistic and flexible goals. Rather than fixating on rigid, linear paths, individuals can outline goals that are adaptive to unforeseen circumstances. This approach allows for a more dynamic response to challenges, acknowledging that the journey may take unexpected turns while maintaining a focus on the ultimate destination.

4. **Build a Supportive Network:** A strong support network is invaluable when navigating life's unexpected twists. Cultivating relationships with individuals who share a similar mindset fosters a sense of community and provides a source of encouragement during challenging times. Whether in personal or professional spheres, a supportive network is instrumental in adopting and sustaining an Option B perspective.

5. **Embrace Failure as a Stepping Stone:** Failure, when viewed through the lens of the Option B perspective, is not a dead-end but a stepping stone toward growth. Individuals can adopt a proactive approach to failure by extracting lessons, adjusting strategies, and viewing setbacks

as opportunities to refine their goals. Embracing failure as a natural part of the journey reduces the fear associated with it and opens the door to transformative experiences.

6. **Practice Cognitive Reframing:** Cognitive reframing is a powerful tool for adopting an Option B perspective. When faced with challenges, individuals can consciously reframe negative thoughts into more positive and constructive interpretations. This process involves questioning automatic assumptions, seeking alternative perspectives, and focusing on the possibilities for growth and learning inherent in every situation.

7. **Encourage Flexibility in Problem-Solving:** Adopting an Option B perspective requires a flexible approach to problem-solving. Rather than becoming fixated on a single solution, individuals can explore multiple alternatives and be open to adjusting their strategies as circumstances evolve. This flexibility enhances adaptability and empowers individuals to navigate challenges with a solution-oriented mindset.

8. **Celebrate Small Wins and Progress:** Acknowledging and celebrating small

wins is essential in maintaining motivation and momentum. By recognizing progress, no matter how incremental, individuals reinforce the idea that challenges are not insurmountable obstacles but opportunities for growth. This practice fosters a positive feedback loop that aligns with the Option B perspective of continuous learning and advancement.

9. **Foster a Culture of Innovation:** In professional settings, adopting an Option B perspective involves fostering a culture of innovation. Encouraging team members to experiment, take calculated risks, and learn from failures contributes to an environment where resilience is valued and adaptive strategies are embraced. This cultural shift promotes a collective mindset that aligns with the principles of Option B.

10. **Seek Mentorship and Learning Opportunities:** Actively seeking mentorship and continuous learning opportunities enhances the adoption of an Option B perspective. Mentors can provide guidance based on their experiences, offering insights into navigating challenges and reframing

setbacks. Engaging in ongoing learning keeps individuals adaptable, curious, and ready to explore alternative paths to success.

Chapter 4: Learning from Setbacks: Transforming Adversity into Advantage

The concept of setbacks as valuable learning experiences

The concept of setbacks as valuable learning experiences is a paradigm shift that reframes the narrative surrounding challenges and failures. Instead of viewing setbacks as roadblocks or indicators of personal inadequacy, this perspective recognizes them as essential components of the learning journey. Setbacks, whether in personal or professional realms, are not the end of the road but rather pivotal moments laden with opportunities for growth, insight, and the development of resilience.

At its core, the exploration of setbacks as valuable learning experiences involves embracing a mindset that sees challenges as dynamic and transformative. Rather than approaching setbacks with a fixed, negative mindset, individuals can choose to view them as catalysts for learning and self-improvement. This shift requires a departure from the fear of failure and a willingness to engage with setbacks as integral aspects of the journey toward personal and professional development.

Setbacks, in this context, become not only acceptable but expected elements of the learning process. They offer a unique vantage point from which individuals can gain invaluable insights into their strengths, weaknesses, and areas for improvement. By reframing setbacks as opportunities for self-reflection and introspection, individuals can extract meaningful lessons that contribute to their ongoing growth.

Furthermore, setbacks provide a reality check that grounds individuals in the complexities of real-world challenges. Success is not always a linear trajectory; setbacks underscore the importance of adaptability and resilience in navigating the twists and turns of personal and professional pursuits. Rather than shying away from setbacks, individuals can use them as compass points, guiding them toward a more informed and nuanced understanding of their goals and aspirations.

The exploration of setbacks as valuable learning experiences also involves a reassessment of the concept of failure. Failure, often stigmatized in society, becomes a dynamic force when viewed through the lens of learning. Instead of representing an endpoint, failure becomes a source of feedback—an indication that adjustments may be needed, strategies reconsidered, or skills further honed. This perspective dismantles the fear associated with failure, fostering a more positive and constructive relationship with setbacks.

In the professional realm, setbacks can be particularly instructive. They offer organizations and individuals alike the chance to recalibrate strategies, innovate, and adapt to an ever-changing landscape. In the face of setbacks, organizations can foster a culture that values experimentation, embraces risk-taking, and recognizes the potential for breakthroughs that often arise from setbacks. The resilience cultivated through setbacks becomes a key asset in navigating the uncertainties of the business environment.

Moreover, setbacks serve as a litmus test for passion and commitment. When individuals encounter challenges that force them to confront their goals and ambitions, the depth of their passion becomes evident. Setbacks become a clarifying force, prompting individuals to reevaluate their aspirations and ensuring that their pursuits align with their authentic selves. In this way, setbacks contribute to a more meaningful and purpose-driven approach to life and work.

Practical strategies for exploring setbacks as valuable learning experiences involve intentional reflection and a commitment to continuous improvement. Rather than dwelling on the negative emotions associated with setbacks, individuals can channel their energy into analyzing the situation objectively. What went wrong? What factors contributed to the setback? What can be learned from this experience? Answering these questions provides a roadmap for turning setbacks into stepping stones for future success.

Additionally, seeking feedback from setbacks can be a powerful tool for learning and growth. Feedback, whether from oneself or from others, helps to pinpoint areas that require attention and adjustment. This feedback loop contributes to an ongoing cycle of improvement, reinforcing the idea that setbacks are not final judgments but rather signposts on the journey toward mastery.

Case studies and examples of individuals who turned adversity into advantage

The stories of individuals who have turned adversity into advantage stand as powerful testimonials to the transformative power of resilience, determination, and a positive mindset. These case studies and examples serve as beacons of inspiration, illustrating how challenges, setbacks, and hardships can be reframed into opportunities for growth, success, and even profound societal impact.

One notable example is Oprah Winfrey, whose early life was marked by adversity and hardship. Growing up in poverty and facing numerous challenges, including abuse and discrimination, Oprah refused to let her circumstances define her. She transformed her difficult past into a source of motivation and resilience. Through hard work, tenacity, and a commitment to continuous learning, Oprah became one of the most influential media personalities and philanthropists in the world. Her ability to turn personal adversity into a platform for success has inspired millions globally.

Another compelling case study is that of J.K. Rowling, the author of the immensely popular Harry Potter series. Before achieving literary success, Rowling faced numerous setbacks, including financial struggles, the death of her mother, and a difficult divorce. However, she used these challenges as fuel for her creativity and perseverance. The rejection of her manuscript by multiple publishers did not deter her; instead, it became a stepping stone to success. Rowling's ability to turn personal adversity into literary triumph is a testament to the resilience of the human spirit.

In the realm of business and entrepreneurship, the story of Elon Musk stands out as a striking example of turning adversity into advantage. Musk faced numerous setbacks and financial challenges throughout his career, including the brink of bankruptcy with his companies Tesla and SpaceX. Despite the odds, Musk remained resilient and unwavering in his pursuit of transformative technologies. Today, he is a visionary entrepreneur and one of the most influential figures in the fields of electric vehicles, space exploration, and renewable energy.

Malala Yousafzai, the Pakistani education advocate and Nobel laureate, is another poignant example. Malala faced adversity at a young age when the Taliban targeted her for advocating girls' education. Despite a life-threatening attack, she emerged stronger, using her experience to amplify her advocacy on a global scale. Malala's resilience and courage turned a personal tragedy into a powerful force for change, making her a symbol of hope and education for girls worldwide.

The medical field offers examples of individuals who turned personal adversity into groundbreaking achievements. Dr. Paul Farmer, co-founder of Partners In Health, faced adversity early in his medical career when he encountered systemic barriers to providing healthcare in impoverished communities. Instead of succumbing to the challenges, Farmer turned them into a catalyst for change. He pioneered innovative approaches to deliver healthcare to the most vulnerable populations, demonstrating how adversity can lead to transformative solutions.

Closer to the world of sports, Michael Jordan's story is a classic example of turning setbacks into legendary success. Jordan faced rejection from his high school basketball team, a setback that fueled his determination to become one of the greatest basketball players of all time. His resilience, work ethic, and ability to turn failures into motivation propelled him to win multiple championships and achieve iconic status in the sports world.

In the technology sector, the story of Steve Jobs provides a compelling narrative of turning adversity into advantage. After being ousted from the company he co-founded, Apple, Jobs faced a period of professional wilderness. However, he used this time to start new ventures and develop new skills. His eventual return to Apple marked a historic turnaround for the company, leading to the creation of groundbreaking products like the iPhone and iPad. Jobs' ability to bounce back from adversity and leverage it for future success showcases the transformative potential within setbacks.

These case studies collectively emphasize the idea that adversity can be a catalyst for personal and professional growth. The individuals mentioned not only overcame challenges but used their experiences as sources of inspiration, innovation, and positive change. Their stories underscore the importance of resilience, a growth mindset, and the belief that setbacks can be opportunities in disguise.

In examining these examples, common themes emerge: an unwavering belief in oneself, a refusal to be defined by adversity, and a commitment to using challenges as stepping stones toward success. These individuals demonstrate that adversity, when faced with courage and resilience, can be a powerful force for personal and societal advancement. Their stories serve as guiding lights for those navigating their own challenges, showing that turning adversity into advantage is not only possible but can lead to remarkable achievements and lasting impact.

Provide guidance on extracting lessons and wisdom from life's challenges

Extracting lessons and wisdom from life's challenges is an art that requires introspection, resilience, and a commitment to personal growth. Rather than viewing challenges as mere obstacles, they can be seen as profound opportunities for learning, self-discovery, and the acquisition of valuable insights that contribute to a more meaningful and purposeful life. Here, we delve into guidance on how to extract lessons and wisdom from life's challenges, transforming adversity into a source of personal and intellectual enrichment.

1. **Cultivate Self-Reflection:** The first step in extracting lessons from life's challenges is to engage in deliberate self-reflection. This involves taking the time to introspectively examine the challenge, the emotions it elicited, and the thought processes that accompanied it. By gaining a deeper understanding of one's reactions and responses, individuals can uncover underlying beliefs, values, and patterns that contribute to personal growth.

2. **Identify Patterns and Triggers:** Challenges often reveal recurring patterns and triggers that influence behavior and decision-making. By identifying these patterns, individuals can gain insights into aspects of their lives that may need attention or adjustment. Recognizing triggers allows for proactive responses, empowering individuals to navigate similar challenges with greater

self-awareness and emotional intelligence.

3. **Focus on the Process, Not Just the Outcome:** In the pursuit of extracting lessons, it's crucial to focus on the process of navigating challenges, not just the outcome. The journey itself holds valuable insights into resilience, adaptability, and the strategies employed. By examining the steps taken, the decisions made, and the lessons learned along the way, individuals can distill wisdom that transcends the specific challenge.

4. **Embrace a Growth Mindset:** Adopting a growth mindset is instrumental in extracting lessons from challenges. Embrace the belief that challenges are opportunities for learning and growth, rather than fixed indicators of success or failure. A growth mindset encourages individuals to view setbacks as stepping stones, fostering a positive and constructive approach to life's difficulties.

5. **Seek Diverse Perspectives:** Extracting lessons from challenges can be enriched by seeking diverse perspectives. Engage in conversations with trusted friends, mentors, or advisors to gain insights that

may not be immediately apparent. Other perspectives can provide valuable angles of analysis, broadening the understanding of the challenge and offering alternative ways to approach and overcome similar obstacles in the future.

6. **Document the Experience:** Keeping a journal or documenting the experience in some form allows for a tangible record of the challenge and the lessons learned. Writing about emotions, thoughts, and the evolving understanding of the situation provides a retrospective lens. Returning to these reflections over time provides a valuable opportunity to track personal growth and revisit the wisdom gained.

7. **Practice Mindfulness:** Mindfulness, the practice of being present in the moment without judgment, enhances the ability to extract lessons from challenges. By approaching challenges with a mindful mindset, individuals can observe their thoughts and emotions without being overwhelmed by them. This awareness creates space for clarity, enabling a more objective and constructive analysis of the lessons embedded in the challenge.

8. **Acknowledge and Accept Imperfection:** Extracting lessons from challenges requires acknowledging and accepting imperfection. Perfectionism often hinders the ability to learn and grow from setbacks. Embrace the idea that challenges are inherent to the human experience, and imperfection is a natural part of the learning journey. This mindset shift reduces the fear of failure and fosters a more open and adaptive approach to challenges.

9. **Celebrate Small Wins:** Recognizing and celebrating small victories along the way contributes to the extraction of lessons and wisdom. Life's challenges are often multifaceted, and progress may come in incremental steps. By acknowledging small wins, individuals reinforce positive behaviors, build confidence, and cultivate a mindset that focuses on continuous improvement.

10. **Apply Lessons to Future Challenges:** The ultimate test of extracting lessons lies in applying newfound wisdom to future challenges. Actively integrating lessons learned into decision-making and problem-solving processes enhances adaptability and resilience. By

consciously applying insights gained from previous challenges, individuals forge a path of continuous learning and growth.

Chapter 5: Thriving Amidst Change: Adapting to Life's Dynamic Nature

The inevitability of change and the importance of adaptability

The inevitability of change is a fundamental aspect of the human experience and the dynamic nature of the world we inhabit. From personal circumstances to societal shifts, change is a constant force that shapes our lives. Recognizing this inevitability is crucial, as it underscores the importance of adaptability—the ability to adjust, evolve, and thrive in the face of ongoing transformation. Embracing change and cultivating adaptability are not just survival skills; they are the keys to unlocking opportunities, fostering resilience, and navigating the complexities of an ever-changing landscape.

Change is woven into the fabric of life, manifesting in various forms such as career transitions, relationship dynamics, technological advancements, and global events. The unpredictability of these changes necessitates a mindset that views them not as disruptions but as integral aspects of growth and progress. Resisting change often leads to stagnation and missed opportunities, whereas embracing it opens doors to new possibilities and experiences.

Adaptability, then, becomes a cornerstone of navigating the inevitability of change. It is the capacity to respond effectively to shifting circumstances, adjusting one's mindset, strategies, and behaviors accordingly. The importance of adaptability is underscored by its role in promoting personal and professional success. Individuals who embrace change with adaptability as their guiding principle are better equipped to overcome challenges, seize opportunities, and thrive in dynamic environments.

In the professional realm, adaptability is increasingly recognized as a critical skill in the face of technological advancements, market fluctuations, and the evolving nature of industries. Companies that prioritize adaptability among their employees foster a culture of innovation and resilience. Employees who demonstrate adaptability are not only better positioned to weather uncertainties but also contribute to organizational growth by bringing fresh perspectives and creative solutions.

Moreover, the inevitability of change extends to the broader context of societal and global dynamics. Social, economic, and environmental changes have profound impacts on communities and individuals. Those who recognize the inevitability of these changes and adapt to new norms, challenges, and opportunities are better positioned to contribute meaningfully to societal progress and navigate the complexities of a rapidly evolving world.

The pace of technological innovation exemplifies the constant flux that characterizes the modern era. In a world where technological advancements shape industries and redefine the way we live and work, adaptability becomes a key determinant of success. Individuals who embrace technological change, upskill when necessary, and leverage emerging technologies are better equipped to thrive in the digital landscape.

Adaptability is also integral to personal development and well-being. Life is a journey marked by various stages, each demanding a capacity to adapt to new roles, responsibilities, and circumstances. Whether it be transitioning to parenthood, navigating changes in health, or adjusting to shifts in personal relationships, adaptability allows individuals to approach these life transitions with resilience and a positive mindset.

Furthermore, adaptability is closely linked to emotional intelligence—a crucial skill in interpersonal relationships. Individuals who can adapt to the emotions and needs of others, navigate conflicts with flexibility, and communicate effectively in diverse contexts build stronger connections and contribute to the harmonious functioning of social structures.

In practical terms, developing adaptability involves cultivating certain traits and practices. A willingness to learn, openness to new ideas, and a proactive approach to problem-solving are all components of adaptability. Embracing a growth mindset, which sees challenges as opportunities for learning and development, is foundational to adaptability. Continuous learning, seeking feedback, and staying curious are habits that support ongoing adaptability in the face of change.

Strategies for thriving amidst life's dynamic nature
Thriving amidst life's dynamic nature requires a holistic approach that encompasses various strategies aimed at fostering resilience, embracing change, and finding fulfillment in the ebb and flow of life's challenges and opportunities. The dynamic nature of life is inevitable, and thriving within it involves not just surviving but actively engaging with the

complexities and uncertainties that arise. Here, we explore strategies that empower individuals to navigate life's dynamic nature with grace, purpose, and a sense of well-being.

1. **Cultivate Resilience:** Resilience is the cornerstone of thriving in the face of life's dynamic nature. Cultivating resilience involves developing the capacity to bounce back from setbacks, adapt to change, and maintain a positive mindset in the midst of challenges. Building resilience is an ongoing process that involves embracing difficulties as opportunities for growth, learning from experiences, and developing a mindset that views setbacks as temporary and surmountable.

2. **Embrace a Growth Mindset:** Central to thriving amidst life's dynamic nature is adopting a growth mindset. This mindset sees challenges as opportunities for learning and development rather than insurmountable obstacles. Embracing a growth mindset involves viewing one's abilities as malleable, being open to new experiences, and understanding that personal and professional growth is an evolving journey rather than a destination.

3. **Cultivate Mindfulness Practices:**
   Mindfulness practices, such as meditation
   and mindful breathing, provide tools for
   staying present in the moment and
   managing stress in the face of life's
   uncertainties. Cultivating mindfulness
   enhances self-awareness, emotional
   regulation, and the ability to navigate
   challenges with clarity and composure.
   Incorporating mindfulness into daily
   routines contributes to a sense of balance
   and well-being.

4. **Build a Supportive Network:** Thriving in
   dynamic life situations is significantly
   influenced by the strength of one's
   support network. Building connections
   with supportive friends, family, and
   mentors provides a valuable foundation
   for emotional and practical assistance. A
   supportive network offers perspectives,
   encouragement, and a sense of belonging,
   fostering resilience and helping
   individuals navigate life's ups and downs.

5. **Set Realistic and Flexible Goals:** Setting
   goals is integral to thriving, but it is
   essential to make them both realistic and
   flexible. Life's dynamic nature often
   requires adjustments to plans and
   expectations. By setting goals that are

adaptive to changing circumstances, individuals can maintain a sense of direction while being open to new possibilities and opportunities that may arise along the way.

6. **Prioritize Self-Care:** Thriving in dynamic environments necessitates prioritizing self-care. This includes attending to physical, mental, and emotional well-being through practices such as regular exercise, adequate sleep, healthy nutrition, and activities that bring joy and relaxation. Self-care is not a luxury but a fundamental aspect of maintaining the energy and resilience needed to navigate life's fluctuations.

7. **Cultivate Adaptability:** Adaptability is a key skill for thriving in dynamic situations. This involves being open to change, quickly adjusting to new circumstances, and viewing challenges as opportunities for innovation and growth. Cultivating adaptability requires a willingness to learn, a proactive approach to problem-solving, and a mindset that sees change as a natural and potentially enriching aspect of life.

8. **Develop Effective Time Management:** Thriving amidst life's dynamic nature

requires effective time management. Prioritizing tasks, setting boundaries, and allocating time to activities that align with personal and professional goals contribute to a sense of control and accomplishment. Effective time management allows individuals to navigate the dynamic nature of responsibilities and pursuits without feeling overwhelmed.

9. **Cultivate Emotional Intelligence:** Emotional intelligence is a vital skill for thriving in diverse and dynamic social environments. Understanding and managing one's own emotions, as well as empathizing with others, enhances interpersonal relationships and contributes to effective communication. Cultivating emotional intelligence fosters resilience, adaptability, and positive connections with those around us.

10. **Practice Gratitude:** Incorporating gratitude into daily life is a powerful strategy for thriving amidst life's dynamic nature. Taking time to reflect on and appreciate the positive aspects of life, even in the midst of challenges, cultivates a positive mindset. Gratitude fosters resilience by shifting the focus from what

is lacking to what is present, creating a foundation for a more fulfilling and optimistic outlook.

Insights into cultivating a mindset that embraces and even welcomes change

Cultivating a mindset that embraces and even welcomes change is a transformative journey that involves shifting perspectives, fostering adaptability, and developing a proactive approach to life's fluctuations. Instead of viewing change as a disruptive force, individuals can embrace it as a catalyst for growth, innovation, and personal development. Insights into cultivating such a mindset involve a combination of self-awareness, intentional practices, and a willingness to see change not as a threat but as an integral part of the human experience.

1. **Embrace a Growth Mindset:** At the core of cultivating a change-embracing mindset is adopting a growth mindset. This mindset, as proposed by psychologist Carol Dweck, sees abilities and intelligence as qualities that can be developed through dedication and effort. Individuals with a growth mindset view challenges and setbacks as opportunities to learn and improve rather than as fixed

indicators of their capabilities. Embracing a growth mindset lays the foundation for welcoming change as a pathway to continuous learning and personal development.

2. **Challenge the Fear of the Unknown:** Fear of the unknown is a common barrier to embracing change. Cultivating a change-welcoming mindset involves challenging this fear by reframing the unknown as a realm of possibilities and opportunities. Instead of fixating on potential risks, individuals can focus on the potential for discovery, learning, and positive outcomes that change can bring. Acknowledging that the unknown is a natural part of life's journey allows for a more open and optimistic approach to change.

3. **Cultivate Curiosity:** Curiosity is a powerful force that propels individuals to explore, learn, and adapt. Cultivating a mindset that welcomes change involves fostering curiosity about the world and oneself. Asking questions, seeking new experiences, and approaching situations with a sense of wonder contribute to a mindset that views change as an exciting avenue for exploration. Curiosity shifts

the focus from apprehension to a proactive engagement with the evolving nature of life.

4. **Recognize Change as a Constant:** Change is an inherent aspect of the human experience, and recognizing it as a constant rather than an exception is key to developing a change-welcoming mindset. Rather than resisting change, individuals can acknowledge that it is an inevitable and natural part of life. This recognition enables a mental shift from a mindset of control and predictability to one that embraces the dynamic and evolving nature of existence.

5. **Focus on the Process, Not Just the Outcome:** Embracing change involves shifting the focus from the end result to the process itself. Often, individuals are fixated on achieving specific outcomes, and any deviation is perceived as a threat. Cultivating a mindset that welcomes change requires valuing the journey, the learning experiences, and the personal growth that occur along the way. By appreciating the process, individuals become more adaptable and open to the changes that unfold.

6. **Learn from Past Experiences:** Reflecting on past experiences of change provides valuable insights into one's ability to adapt and navigate uncertainties. Individuals can draw on their resilience and resourcefulness demonstrated in previous situations of change. Analyzing past experiences allows for the identification of strategies that were effective and encourages the development of a repertoire of coping mechanisms, contributing to a more positive outlook on future changes.

7. **Develop Flexibility in Thinking:** Rigidity in thinking is a common obstacle to embracing change. Developing flexibility in thinking involves being open to alternative perspectives, considering different possibilities, and adapting one's mental frameworks. Embracing change often requires letting go of preconceived notions and embracing a mindset that is receptive to new ideas, approaches, and ways of living.

8. **Cultivate a Positive Relationship with Uncertainty:** Uncertainty is an inherent part of change, and cultivating a positive relationship with it is essential for a change-welcoming mindset. Rather than

fearing uncertainty, individuals can see it as an opportunity for creativity, innovation, and new beginnings. Approaching uncertainty with a positive mindset allows individuals to navigate change with resilience and an optimistic outlook.

9. **Set Realistic Expectations:** Unrealistic expectations can contribute to resistance towards change. Cultivating a change-welcoming mindset involves setting realistic expectations and understanding that not all changes will be smooth or immediate. Recognizing that change is a gradual process allows individuals to approach it with patience and a more positive attitude.

10. **Practice Mindfulness and Presence:** Mindfulness practices, such as meditation and being present in the moment, are powerful tools for cultivating a mindset that welcomes change. Mindfulness fosters awareness of thoughts and emotions, allowing individuals to respond to change with greater clarity and composure. Being present in the current moment reduces anxiety about the future and enhances the ability to adapt to changing circumstances.

In conclusion, cultivating a mindset that embraces and even welcomes change is a transformative journey that involves intentional shifts in thinking and perspective. By adopting a growth mindset, challenging the fear of the unknown, cultivating curiosity, recognizing change as a constant, focusing on the process, learning from past experiences, developing flexibility in thinking, cultivating a positive relationship with uncertainty, setting realistic expectations, and practicing mindfulness, individuals can develop a resilient and proactive approach to life's dynamic nature. Embracing change becomes not just a necessity but an opportunity for continuous learning, growth, and the enrichment of the human experience.

Chapter 6: Finding Purpose in Adversity: Beyond Survival to Meaning

Concept of finding purpose in the midst of adversity

Exploring the concept of finding purpose in the midst of adversity delves into the profound capacity of individuals to derive meaning and direction even when faced with challenges. Adversity, often seen as a test of resilience, can become a transformative force, leading individuals to discover a deeper sense of purpose and meaning in their lives. This exploration involves understanding how adversity can be a catalyst for introspection, growth, and the redirection of one's life toward a more purposeful and fulfilling trajectory.

Adversity, in its various forms, has the potential to shake the foundations of individuals' lives. Whether it be personal setbacks, health crises, or unforeseen challenges, the experience of adversity often prompts a reevaluation of priorities and a search for meaning. Instead of succumbing to despair, individuals may embark on a journey to uncover a sense of purpose that transcends the immediate difficulties they face.

One aspect of finding purpose in adversity is the process of introspection. Adversity often compels individuals to reflect on their values, aspirations, and the overall trajectory of their lives. Through introspection, individuals can identify core beliefs and passions that may have been obscured by the routine of daily life. This reflective process serves as a compass, guiding individuals toward a clearer understanding of what truly matters to them and what they want to contribute to the world.

Growth in the midst of adversity is another pathway to discovering purpose. The challenges faced during difficult times can be transformative, fostering personal development, resilience, and a newfound awareness of one's strengths. As individuals navigate and overcome adversity, they may unearth untapped potentials, strengths, and capacities that were dormant or underestimated. This self-discovery can be instrumental in shaping a renewed sense of purpose that aligns more authentically with who they are becoming through the adversities they endure.

Furthermore, finding purpose in adversity often involves a shift in perspective. Rather than viewing challenges as insurmountable obstacles, individuals may choose to interpret them as opportunities for learning and growth. This shift in mindset is crucial in transforming adversity from a source of despair into a catalyst for positive change. Embracing challenges as integral parts of the journey allows individuals to extract meaning from their experiences, propelling them toward a purpose that arises from a profound understanding of life's complexities.

The concept of finding purpose in adversity extends beyond personal development to encompass a broader sense of connection and contribution. Individuals may discover a sense of purpose by recognizing the impact they can have on others or on the world at large. Acts of kindness, empathy, and service often take center stage during challenging times, leading individuals to realize that their actions can be meaningful and purposeful, even in the face of adversity.

The narratives of individuals who have found purpose in adversity are replete with stories of resilience and determination. Survivors of life-altering events, advocates for social justice, and individuals who have turned personal hardships into sources of inspiration exemplify the transformative power of finding purpose in adversity. These stories underscore the capacity of the human spirit to not only endure challenges but also to find meaning and purpose in the aftermath.

Moreover, the concept of finding purpose in adversity highlights the dynamic nature of purpose itself. Purpose is not a static destination but an ongoing journey that evolves as individuals navigate the twists and turns of life. Adversity becomes a crucible for refining and reshaping one's sense of purpose, encouraging individuals to remain open to continuous growth and discovery.

In conclusion, exploring the concept of finding purpose in the midst of adversity reveals the profound and transformative nature of human resilience. Adversity, rather than being a roadblock, becomes a crucible for self-discovery, growth, and the revelation of a deeper sense of purpose. The journey of finding purpose in adversity involves introspection, personal development, a shift in perspective, and a recognition of the interconnectedness of one's life with the lives of others. Ultimately, the stories of those who have found purpose in the face of adversity illuminate the indomitable spirit of the human experience and its capacity to turn challenges into opportunities for profound meaning and fulfillment.

The transformative power of aligning personal goals with a sense of purpose

The transformative power of aligning personal goals with a sense of purpose lies in the profound synergy that occurs when individuals connect their aspirations with a deeper, intrinsic meaning. Purpose acts as a guiding force that infuses goals with significance, providing a source of motivation, resilience, and fulfillment. This alignment transcends mere achievement, fostering a holistic sense of well-being and contributing to a more meaningful and purposeful life.

When personal goals are aligned with a sense of purpose, they become more than just benchmarks or accomplishments; they become stepping stones in a larger journey toward a fulfilling and meaningful life. Purpose serves as the North Star, guiding individuals through the complexities of decision-making, shaping their priorities, and influencing the choices they make in pursuit of their goals.

One of the transformative aspects of aligning personal goals with purpose is the enhanced motivation it provides. Goals infused with purpose carry a deeper intrinsic value, igniting a passion and commitment that transcends external rewards. Individuals are more likely to persevere through challenges, setbacks, and obstacles when their goals are rooted in a sense of purpose. This sustained motivation is a powerful catalyst for personal growth and achievement.

Moreover, aligning personal goals with purpose contributes to a heightened sense of resilience. When setbacks occur, individuals driven by a sense of purpose are better equipped to bounce back, reevaluate, and adapt. The connection to a larger, meaningful narrative provides a foundation for navigating the inevitable challenges that accompany the pursuit of goals. This resilience not only enables individuals to overcome obstacles but also transforms setbacks into opportunities for learning and refinement.

The transformative power of alignment is also evident in the holistic impact on well-being. Goals that are aligned with purpose contribute to a sense of fulfillment and satisfaction that extends beyond mere success or achievement. Individuals experience a deeper connection to their actions and a greater sense of authenticity, leading to a more balanced and enriched life. This holistic well-being is rooted in the alignment of personal aspirations with a sense of purpose that resonates with one's values and beliefs.

Furthermore, aligning personal goals with purpose fosters a sense of direction and clarity.

Purpose serves as a guiding principle that helps individuals discern between what is truly meaningful and what may be distractions or detours. This clarity in goal-setting facilitates a more focused and intentional approach to personal and professional endeavors. As a result, individuals are better able to allocate their time, energy, and resources in ways that align with their broader sense of purpose.

The transformative power of alignment extends beyond individual well-being to encompass a positive ripple effect on relationships and communities. Individuals who are aligned with their purpose often contribute to a more cohesive and harmonious social fabric. Their actions are driven by a deeper understanding of how personal goals can contribute to the well-being of others and the greater good. This sense of interconnected purpose fosters collaboration, empathy, and a shared commitment to collective flourishing.

Furthermore, the transformative impact of alignment is evident in the sustained motivation for continuous growth and development. Individuals with aligned goals and purpose are more likely to view their journey as an ongoing process of self-discovery and improvement. The pursuit of excellence becomes not just a destination but a lifelong commitment to evolving, learning, and contributing positively to the world.

In conclusion, the transformative power of aligning personal goals with a sense of purpose is a dynamic and enriching journey. Purpose infuses goals with intrinsic motivation, resilience, and a holistic sense of well-being. This alignment not only propels individuals toward their aspirations but also fosters personal growth, fulfillment, and positive contributions to the broader community. The transformative synergy of purpose-driven goals transcends the conventional notion of success, offering a more profound and meaningful way of navigating the complexities of life.

Exercises and reflections to help uncover their sense of purpose in challenging times

Uncovering a sense of purpose in challenging times requires intentional reflection and self-discovery. The journey to finding purpose amidst adversity involves a series of exercises and reflections designed to tap into one's values, passions, and aspirations. These exercises provide a roadmap for individuals to navigate the complexities of challenging circumstances and emerge with a clearer understanding of their purpose. Here are some exercises and reflections to guide readers on this transformative journey:

1. **Values Clarification:** Start by identifying and clarifying your core values. List the principles and beliefs that are most important to you. Reflect on times when you felt most aligned with these values. During challenging times, aligning with your core values can provide a sense of stability and direction.

2. **Life Review:** Conduct a life review by examining significant moments, achievements, and challenges throughout your life. Identify patterns, themes, and recurring interests. Explore how past experiences have shaped your values and priorities. This retrospective analysis can unveil insights into your overarching purpose.

3. **Passion Inventory:** Create a passion inventory by listing activities or pursuits that bring you joy and fulfillment. Consider both past and present interests. Reflect on why these activities resonate with you. Connecting with your passions can illuminate aspects of your purpose that may have been overshadowed by challenges.

4. **Strengths Assessment:** Take an inventory of your strengths and skills. Consider both tangible and intangible

strengths. Reflect on how you can leverage these strengths to navigate challenges and contribute to the well-being of yourself and others. Your unique capabilities can be integral to your sense of purpose.

5. **Impact Reflection:** Reflect on the impact you want to have on the world or the lives of others. Consider the positive changes you aspire to make, both big and small. Visualize the kind of legacy you want to leave. This exercise encourages a forward-looking perspective, aligning your goals with a broader sense of purpose.

6. **Journaling Prompts:** Use journaling as a tool for self-reflection. Write about your experiences during challenging times, exploring the emotions, lessons learned, and personal growth. Use prompts like "What brings me joy?" or "What kind of impact do I want to make?" to delve into the layers of your purpose.

7. **Vision Board Creation:** Construct a vision board using images, words, and symbols that resonate with your aspirations and values. This visual representation can serve as a daily reminder of your sense of purpose.

Update the vision board periodically, allowing it to evolve along with your understanding of purpose.

8. **Mentorship Exploration:** Seek guidance from mentors or individuals you admire. Engage in conversations that explore their sense of purpose and how they have navigated challenges. Learn from their experiences and consider how their insights align with or inspire your own sense of purpose.

9. **Future Self Visualization:** Envision your future self in vivid detail. Imagine the person you aspire to become, the contributions you want to make, and the impact you hope to have. This exercise taps into the aspirational dimension of purpose, helping you set goals that align with your evolving sense of self.

10. **Mindfulness and Meditation:** Practice mindfulness and meditation to cultivate a quiet space for reflection. Mindfulness allows you to observe your thoughts and emotions without judgment, creating mental clarity. In moments of stillness, insights about your purpose may naturally emerge.

11. **Community Engagement:** Engage with your community or volunteer for a cause you believe in. Actively participating in activities that align with your values provides real-world experiences that can illuminate your sense of purpose. The impact of your contributions may further clarify your goals.

12. **Feedback Seeking:** Seek feedback from friends, family, or colleagues. Ask them about your strengths, the positive impact you've had on them, and the qualities they admire. External perspectives can provide valuable insights that complement your self-reflection.

13. **Limiting Beliefs Exploration:** Identify and challenge any limiting beliefs that may hinder your pursuit of purpose. Explore thoughts that undermine your confidence or sense of worth. Transforming limiting beliefs into empowering affirmations can create a more conducive mindset for purpose discovery.

In conclusion, uncovering a sense of purpose in challenging times is a nuanced and personal journey. These exercises and reflections are designed to guide readers through a process of self-discovery, introspection, and intentional goal-setting. By engaging in these activities, individuals can navigate the complexities of adversity with a clearer understanding of their values, passions, and aspirations, ultimately unveiling a sense of purpose that transcends the challenges they face.

Chapter 7: Building Support Systems: The Power of Connection in Difficult Times

Importance of building strong support systems during challenging times

The importance of building strong support systems during challenging times cannot be overstated. These systems, comprising friends, family, mentors, and even communities, serve as a crucial foundation for emotional well-being, resilience, and the ability to navigate adversity effectively. In the face of life's trials, having a robust support network can make a significant difference in one's ability to cope, adapt, and emerge stronger from difficult circumstances.

First and foremost, strong support systems provide a vital source of emotional sustenance. Challenging times often bring forth a range of emotions, including stress, anxiety, and even despair. Having individuals who can offer empathy, understanding, and a listening ear creates a safe space for expressing and processing these emotions. Emotional support not only alleviates the burden of facing difficulties alone but also contributes to mental and psychological resilience.

In addition to emotional support, strong support systems offer practical assistance. During challenging times, individuals may find themselves grappling with various responsibilities and tasks. A well-established support network can help share the load, providing tangible assistance such as childcare, meal preparation, or even financial support. This collaborative effort eases the strain on individuals facing challenges, allowing them to focus on coping and recovery.

Moreover, support systems serve as a reality check and a source of diverse perspectives. When navigating difficult situations, individuals may find it challenging to see beyond their immediate circumstances. Trusted friends, family members, or mentors can offer fresh insights, alternative viewpoints, and valuable advice. This diversity of perspectives can be instrumental in problem-solving and decision-making during challenging times.

Building strong support systems fosters a sense of belonging and connectedness. The knowledge that there are people who care, understand, and stand by during tough times contributes to a profound sense of security. This sense of belonging is a powerful antidote to feelings of isolation and loneliness that often accompany challenges. It reinforces the understanding that individuals are not alone in their struggles.

Moreover, support systems play a crucial role in preserving mental health. The stigma surrounding mental health issues can be a barrier to seeking professional help. In such cases, friends and family who provide non-judgmental support can encourage individuals to prioritize their mental well-being. This support can be a crucial first step in seeking professional assistance if needed, contributing to a comprehensive approach to mental health care.

Strong support systems also contribute to resilience by fostering a culture of mutual encouragement and motivation. In times of adversity, individuals may face self-doubt and a sense of hopelessness. Encouragement from a supportive network can reignite a sense of purpose and belief in one's ability to overcome challenges. The collective strength derived from shared experiences and mutual support enhances resilience and the capacity to bounce back from setbacks.

Furthermore, building support systems promotes a culture of reciprocity and compassion. Individuals who have experienced support during their challenging times are often more inclined to offer support to others in need. This cycle of reciprocity strengthens communities and contributes to the overall well-being of society. It emphasizes the importance of interdependence and collective resilience in the face of life's uncertainties.

In a professional context, strong support systems are equally valuable. Colleagues, mentors, and a supportive work environment contribute to a sense of security and confidence. This, in turn, enhances an individual's ability to navigate professional challenges, fostering creativity, collaboration, and productivity even in the midst of uncertainty.

In conclusion, the importance of building strong support systems during challenging times cannot be overstated. These networks provide emotional sustenance, practical assistance, diverse perspectives, a sense of belonging, and contribute to mental health and resilience. Whether in personal or professional spheres, the collective strength derived from a supportive network is a powerful resource that empowers individuals to face adversity with greater fortitude, adaptability, and a sense of interconnectedness. Assembling and nurturing these support systems is an investment in well-being that pays dividends during life's most challenging moments.

The impact of connection and community on individual resilience

The impact of connection and community on individual resilience is a profound and transformative force that shapes the ability to navigate challenges, adapt to adversity, and find strength in the face of uncertainty. The human experience is inherently social, and the power of connection, whether with friends, family, or a broader community, plays a crucial role in bolstering individual resilience.

At its core, connection provides a sturdy foundation for emotional well-being. In times of difficulty, having a network of supportive relationships allows individuals to express and process their emotions. Whether it's sharing joys or confiding fears, the act of connecting with others creates a space where emotions can be acknowledged, validated, and shared. This emotional support becomes a cornerstone of resilience, helping individuals weather the storms of life with a sense of understanding and compassion.

Moreover, the impact of connection on resilience is evident in the sense of belonging that communities foster. Humans are social beings, and a feeling of belonging is fundamental to mental and emotional health. Communities provide a sense of identity, purpose, and shared values, offering individuals a place where they are accepted and understood. This sense of belonging is a powerful source of comfort and stability, contributing significantly to an individual's capacity to bounce back from adversity.

Communities also play a crucial role in providing practical support during challenging times. From tangible assistance such as helping with daily tasks to offering financial support, the collective strength of a community can alleviate the burden of individual challenges. This collaborative effort not only lightens the load but also reinforces the understanding that individuals are not isolated in their struggles. The reciprocity of support within a community creates a safety net that bolsters individual resilience by fostering interdependence.

The impact of connection and community on resilience is particularly evident in shared experiences. When individuals face challenges collectively, the sense of solidarity enhances resilience. Shared experiences create a sense of universality, reminding individuals that they are not alone in their struggles. This shared resilience is often amplified during times of crisis, emphasizing the strength derived from collective support and a shared sense of purpose.

Furthermore, the impact of connection extends beyond immediate relationships to the broader community fabric. Engaging with a community, whether local or virtual, exposes individuals to diverse perspectives, experiences, and coping strategies. The exchange of ideas and the sharing of wisdom within a community contribute to a collective resilience that goes beyond individual capacities. The knowledge that others have faced similar challenges and emerged stronger creates a reservoir of inspiration and guidance.

In a world that can sometimes feel isolating, the impact of connection on resilience is a beacon of hope. It provides individuals with a network of allies who can offer guidance, encouragement, and practical assistance. The act of reaching out and connecting with others fosters a sense of empowerment, reminding individuals that they have a support system to rely on during difficult times.

Moreover, the impact of connection on resilience is not confined to personal relationships. In a professional context, a sense of connection within a workplace or industry community contributes to individual and collective resilience. Professional networks provide opportunities for collaboration, mentorship, and the sharing of best practices. The support and camaraderie within professional communities enhance an individual's ability to navigate challenges in the ever-evolving landscape of work.

In conclusion, the impact of connection and community on individual resilience is multi-faceted and profound. Whether in personal or professional spheres, the bonds formed through connection provide emotional support, practical assistance, a sense of belonging, and shared resilience. The collective strength derived from a network of relationships empowers individuals to face challenges with greater fortitude, adaptability, and a sense of shared purpose. Nurturing and investing in these connections is an essential aspect of building personal and collective resilience in the complex tapestry of life.

Practical tips for cultivating and maintaining meaningful connections

Cultivating and maintaining meaningful connections is a transformative endeavor that contributes significantly to overall well-being and a sense of fulfillment. In a world that is increasingly interconnected yet often characterized by superficial interactions, intentional efforts are essential to foster genuine connections. Here are practical tips to guide individuals in cultivating and sustaining meaningful connections in various aspects of life:

1. **Prioritize Active Listening:** Actively listening is a cornerstone of meaningful connections. When engaged in conversations, focus on the speaker, show genuine interest, and avoid distractions. Reflecting back what you've heard demonstrates understanding and reinforces the connection by acknowledging the other person's thoughts and feelings.

2. **Practice Empathy:** Cultivate empathy by putting yourself in others' shoes. Understanding and resonating with their emotions fosters a deeper connection. Ask open-ended questions that invite individuals to share their experiences, and respond with compassion. Demonstrating empathy builds trust and strengthens the foundation of meaningful relationships.

3. **Show Authenticity:** Authenticity is key to cultivating genuine connections. Be true to yourself and share your thoughts, feelings, and experiences openly. Authenticity creates an atmosphere of trust, encouraging others to reciprocate

and contribute to a more authentic exchange of ideas and emotions.

4. **Be Present:** In our fast-paced world, being present in the moment is a precious gift. When spending time with others, minimize distractions, put away electronic devices, and focus on the shared experience. Being fully present communicates attentiveness and enhances the quality of connections.

5. **Initiate Meaningful Conversations:** Move beyond small talk by initiating conversations that delve into deeper topics. Explore shared values, dreams, and aspirations. Meaningful conversations contribute to a sense of connection by fostering mutual understanding and creating a space for authentic self-expression.

6. **Celebrate Milestones and Achievements:** Actively participate in the significant moments of others' lives. Celebrate their achievements, milestones, and joys. Recognizing and acknowledging positive events fosters a sense of support and shared happiness, deepening the connection between individuals.

7. **Express Gratitude:** Regularly express gratitude to those who contribute positively to your life. A simple thank-you, whether verbal or written, goes a long way in affirming the value of the connection. Gratitude creates a positive cycle, reinforcing the bond between individuals.

8. **Create Shared Experiences:** Foster connections by creating shared experiences. Whether through shared activities, adventures, or projects, creating memories together builds a unique bond. Shared experiences create a reservoir of shared history that strengthens the connection over time.

9. **Be Mindful of Non-Verbal Cues:** Pay attention to non-verbal cues such as body language, facial expressions, and tone of voice. Non-verbal communication often conveys emotions and sentiments that words may not capture. Being attuned to these cues deepens the understanding between individuals.

10. **Respect Boundaries:** Respect the boundaries of others and communicate your own boundaries clearly. Understanding and respecting personal space, preferences, and limits contribute

to a healthy and sustainable connection.
Clear communication ensures that the
connection is built on mutual respect and
consideration.

11. **Stay Connected Digitally:** Leverage
    digital platforms to stay connected,
    especially with those who may be
    geographically distant. Regular messages,
    video calls, or even shared digital
    activities help bridge the gap and
    maintain connections in today's
    interconnected world.

12. **Invest Time in Relationships:**
    Meaningful connections require time and
    effort. Schedule regular time for
    interactions, whether in person or
    virtually. Invest in the relationship by
    being consistently present and engaged.

13. **Offer Support During Challenges:** Be a
    source of support during challenging
    times. Offering a listening ear, providing
    practical assistance, or simply expressing
    empathy during difficult moments
    strengthens the connection by
    demonstrating reliability and care.

14. **Be Open to New Connections:** Cultivate
    an openness to new connections. Be
    receptive to meeting new people,

exploring diverse perspectives, and expanding your social circles. Embracing new connections enriches your life and broadens your network of meaningful relationships.

15. **Seek Commonalities:** Identify common interests and values that form the foundation of connections. Shared hobbies, passions, or goals create a sense of camaraderie and deepen the bond between individuals.

In conclusion, cultivating and maintaining meaningful connections is an intentional and ongoing process that requires genuine effort and commitment. By prioritizing active listening, practicing empathy, showing authenticity, being present, initiating meaningful conversations, celebrating achievements, expressing gratitude, creating shared experiences, being mindful of non-verbal cues, respecting boundaries, staying connected digitally, investing time in relationships, offering support during challenges, being open to new connections, and seeking commonalities, individuals can nurture connections that contribute to a richer, more fulfilling life. These practical tips form the building blocks of authentic and lasting relationships that withstand the tests of time and adversity.

Chapter 8: Success Redefined: The Option B Revolution in Action

Real-life examples of individuals who have embraced the Option B Revolution

Real-life examples of individuals who have embraced the Option B Revolution serve as powerful narratives that illuminate the transformative potential of resilience, growth, and redefining success in the face of life's challenges. These individuals embody the principles of the Option B mindset, demonstrating how adversity can be a catalyst for positive change and personal transformation. Their stories inspire and resonate, showcasing the strength of the human spirit in navigating unexpected twists and turns.

One notable example is that of Malala Yousafzai, the Pakistani activist for female education who survived a targeted attack by the Taliban. Malala, undeterred by the violence she faced, emerged as a global advocate for education and women's rights. Her unwavering commitment to her cause, even in the face of adversity, exemplifies the Option B Revolution's core tenets—resilience, the pursuit of purpose, and the ability to turn challenges into opportunities for positive impact.

Another compelling example is the story of Oprah Winfrey, who faced a challenging childhood marked by poverty and adversity. Despite early setbacks, Oprah transcended her circumstances, becoming a media mogul, philanthropist, and influential figure. Her journey reflects the transformative power of resilience and the possibility of redefining success on one's own terms, embodying the essence of the Option B Revolution.

In the realm of business, the story of Howard Schultz, the CEO of Starbucks, provides an inspiring example of embracing alternatives and possibilities. Schultz faced professional setbacks and challenges, including being fired from Starbucks in its early years. However, rather than succumbing to defeat, he returned to transform the company into a global phenomenon. Schultz's journey underscores the Option B Revolution's theme of leveraging setbacks as opportunities for growth and innovation.

The narrative of J.K. Rowling, the author of the Harry Potter series, is another poignant example. Before achieving literary success, Rowling faced personal and financial hardships, including being a single parent living on welfare. Her perseverance in the face of adversity and her ability to channel her experiences into creating one of the most beloved literary franchises demonstrate the transformative potential of resilience and the capacity to find purpose in unexpected places.

In the world of sports, the story of Serena Williams serves as a testament to the Option B Revolution. Williams, despite facing health challenges and setbacks, including life-threatening complications during childbirth, returned to the tennis court with unparalleled determination. Her journey exemplifies the concept of resilience, as she not only overcame physical obstacles but also continued to excel in her professional career.

The example of Nick Vujicic, an Australian motivational speaker born with a rare disorder characterized by the absence of limbs, is a powerful illustration of embracing alternatives and cultivating a mindset that welcomes change. Vujicic's journey from struggling with his identity to inspiring millions with his motivational speeches underscores the transformative power of choosing a positive perspective in the face of adversity.

Additionally, the story of Elizabeth Smart, who survived a harrowing kidnapping ordeal, showcases the psychological aspects of resilience. Smart, through her advocacy work for victims of abduction and sexual assault, illustrates how trauma can be transformed into a source of strength and resilience. Her commitment to empowering others who have faced similar challenges exemplifies the Option B Revolution's emphasis on using personal growth to make a positive impact on the world.

The lives of these individuals highlight that the Option B Revolution is not confined to a specific context but is a universal concept applicable to diverse aspects of life. Whether in education, business, literature, sports, or personal development, these real-life examples demonstrate that embracing alternatives, finding purpose in adversity, and cultivating resilience can lead to profound transformation and impact.

In conclusion, the stories of Malala Yousafzai, Oprah Winfrey, Howard Schultz, J.K. Rowling, Serena Williams, Nick Vujicic, and Elizabeth Smart exemplify the Option B Revolution in action. These individuals have navigated life's challenges with resilience, redefined success on their own terms, and embraced the possibilities that arise from setbacks. Their narratives inspire others to adopt a mindset that welcomes change, turns adversity into advantage, and fosters personal growth in the face of life's unexpected twists. Through their journeys, they have become living testaments to the transformative power of the Option B Revolution.

Varied ways in which success can be redefined in the face of challenges

In the face of challenges, the traditional concept of success undergoes a profound redefinition, acknowledging that success is a multifaceted and subjective construct that extends beyond conventional achievements. The varied ways in which success can be redefined in challenging circumstances highlight the resilience of the human spirit and the capacity to find fulfillment in unexpected places.

One dimension of redefining success involves prioritizing personal growth and self-discovery. Rather than measuring success solely by external markers such as career achievements or material wealth, individuals may shift their focus to inner development. This transformative perspective sees challenges as opportunities for self-reflection, learning, and the discovery of untapped strengths. Success, in this context, becomes synonymous with continuous personal evolution and the realization of one's fullest potential.

Redefining success also involves placing a greater emphasis on well-being and mental health. In challenging times, individuals may reassess their priorities, recognizing that true success encompasses a state of balance and inner peace. This redefinition involves prioritizing self-care, emotional resilience, and the cultivation of healthy relationships. Success, from this perspective, is intrinsically linked to a sense of well-being that goes beyond external achievements and embraces the holistic aspects of a fulfilling life.

Another facet of redefining success involves embracing a more flexible and adaptive mindset. In the face of unexpected challenges, individuals may reevaluate rigid definitions of success that are based on specific outcomes or timelines. Success, in this context, is redefined as the ability to adapt to change, navigate uncertainties, and find innovative solutions to unforeseen problems. Flexibility and adaptability become integral components of a successful approach to life's challenges.

The concept of relational success is another transformative redefinition that emerges in the face of challenges. Rather than focusing solely on individual achievements, individuals may place greater value on the quality of their relationships and connections. Success, from this perspective, is intertwined with the ability to cultivate meaningful connections, provide support to others, and contribute positively to the well-being of the community. Relational success acknowledges the interconnectedness of individuals and underscores the importance of collective thriving.

Furthermore, redefining success may involve a shift towards a more purpose-driven approach to life. In challenging circumstances, individuals may seek a deeper meaning and significance in their endeavors. Success, in this context, is redefined as aligning one's actions with a sense of purpose, contributing to a greater good, and making a positive impact on the world. The pursuit of purpose becomes a guiding force that transcends external measures of success.

Creativity and innovation also play a pivotal role in the redefinition of success. In the face of challenges, individuals may discover new avenues for success by embracing creativity and thinking outside traditional boundaries. Success, from this perspective, is not confined to predetermined paths but involves the exploration of alternative solutions, novel ideas, and innovative approaches. The ability to adapt and innovate becomes a measure of success in its own right.

Moreover, redefining success can encompass the cultivation of resilience and the capacity to bounce back from setbacks. Instead of viewing challenges as obstacles to success, individuals may redefine success as the ability to persevere, learn from adversity, and emerge stronger. Success, in this context, is inseparable from resilience—a dynamic quality that enables individuals to navigate life's complexities with courage and tenacity.

The redefinition of success also embraces a heightened awareness of one's values and the alignment of actions with those values. In challenging times, individuals may reassess what truly matters to them, placing greater emphasis on living in alignment with their core values. Success, from this perspective, is not solely defined by external standards but is deeply rooted in authenticity, integrity, and a sense of congruence with one's values.

In conclusion, the varied ways in which success can be redefined in the face of challenges underscore the dynamic and adaptable nature of this concept. Whether through personal growth, well-being, adaptability, relational success, purpose-driven living, creativity, resilience, or values alignment, individuals navigate challenges by embracing a more nuanced and multifaceted understanding of success. This redefinition reflects the human capacity for growth, adaptation, and the pursuit of fulfillment in the midst of life's uncertainties.

A roadmap to apply the Option B Revolution in their own lives

Applying the Option B Revolution in one's life involves a transformative journey that empowers individuals to navigate challenges, redefine success, and cultivate resilience. This roadmap offers practical steps for readers to integrate the principles of the Option B mindset into their daily lives, fostering personal growth and a positive response to life's unexpected twists.

1. **Embrace a Growth Mindset:** Start by cultivating a growth mindset, recognizing that challenges are opportunities for learning and growth. Embrace the belief that abilities and intelligence can be developed through dedication and hard work. This mindset shift lays the foundation for approaching challenges with a positive and adaptive attitude.

2. **Define Your Values:** Clearly define your values and priorities. Reflect on what truly matters to you, both personally and professionally. Understanding your core values provides a compass for decision-making and goal-setting, aligning your actions with a sense of purpose and authenticity.

3. **Set Realistic Goals:** Establish realistic and achievable goals that align with your

values. Break down larger objectives into smaller, manageable steps. Setting clear goals provides a sense of direction and accomplishment, contributing to a feeling of progress even in the face of challenges.

4. **Cultivate Resilience:** Actively cultivate resilience by reframing setbacks as opportunities for learning and growth. Develop coping strategies to manage stress and adversity. Resilience involves not only bouncing back from challenges but also using them as stepping stones for personal development.

5. **Build a Support Network:** Surround yourself with a strong support network of friends, family, and mentors. Share your experiences, seek guidance, and offer support in return. Building meaningful connections creates a safety net during challenging times and enhances overall well-being.

6. **Practice Self-Compassion:** Be kind to yourself in the face of challenges. Practice self-compassion by acknowledging that everyone encounters difficulties. Treat yourself with the same kindness and understanding that you would offer to a friend facing similar circumstances.

7. **Adopt a Solution-Focused Approach:** Approach challenges with a solution-focused mindset. Instead of dwelling on problems, focus on identifying potential solutions and taking actionable steps. This proactive approach empowers you to navigate challenges with a sense of agency and control.

8. **Foster Flexibility and Adaptability:** Develop flexibility and adaptability in your mindset. Recognize that life is dynamic, and unexpected changes are inevitable. Being adaptable allows you to navigate uncertainties with greater ease and creativity.

9. **Celebrate Progress, Not Just Results:** Shift the focus from purely outcome-based success to celebrating progress and effort. Acknowledge and celebrate small victories along the way. Recognizing your journey fosters a positive mindset and motivates continued growth.

10. **Engage in Continuous Learning:** Cultivate a commitment to continuous learning. View every experience, positive or challenging, as an opportunity to acquire new skills, knowledge, and insights. Embracing a mindset of

continuous learning enhances your adaptability and resilience.

11. **Practice Mindfulness and Reflection:** Incorporate mindfulness and reflection into your daily routine. Create moments of stillness to observe your thoughts and emotions without judgment. Mindfulness enhances self-awareness and contributes to a more intentional and purposeful life.

12. **Explore Alternative Perspectives:** Challenge fixed perspectives by exploring alternative viewpoints. Engage in conversations with diverse individuals, read widely, and expose yourself to different ideas. Embracing a variety of perspectives fosters creativity and a more nuanced understanding of challenges.

13. **Balance Ambition with Self-Care:** Find a balance between pursuing ambitious goals and prioritizing self-care. Recognize the importance of rest, relaxation, and overall well-being in sustaining long-term success. Building a foundation of self-care contributes to resilience and a sustainable approach to challenges.

14. **Express Gratitude Regularly:** Cultivate a habit of expressing gratitude regularly. Take time to acknowledge and appreciate

the positive aspects of your life. Gratitude fosters a positive mindset, enhancing your ability to navigate challenges with a sense of optimism.

15. **Inspire and Support Others:** Pay it forward by inspiring and supporting others on their journeys. Share your experiences, offer guidance, and contribute to the well-being of your community. Creating a supportive environment benefits not only you but also those around you.

In conclusion, applying the Option B Revolution in your life involves a deliberate and continuous commitment to personal growth, resilience, and redefining success. By embracing a growth mindset, defining values, setting realistic goals, cultivating resilience, building a support network, practicing self-compassion, adopting a solution-focused approach, fostering flexibility, celebrating progress, engaging in continuous learning, practicing mindfulness, exploring alternative perspectives, balancing ambition with self-care, expressing gratitude regularly, and inspiring others, you create a roadmap for navigating life's challenges with courage, purpose, and a positive mindset. The Option B Revolution becomes a transformative guide for living a life that not only embraces alternatives and possibilities but also thrives amidst the complexities of the unexpected.

Conclusion: Embracing the Option B Revolution in Your Journey

Key principles and takeaways from the Option B Revolution

The Option B Revolution encapsulates a profound shift in mindset and approach towards life's challenges, emphasizing resilience, growth, and the redefinition of success. Summarizing key principles and takeaways from this transformative concept provides a comprehensive understanding of how individuals can navigate adversity, embrace alternatives, and foster personal development.

1. **Resilience as a Foundation:** At the core of the Option B Revolution lies the principle of resilience. Rather than viewing challenges as insurmountable obstacles, individuals are encouraged to cultivate resilience—a dynamic quality that enables them to bounce back from setbacks, learn from adversity, and emerge stronger. Resilience becomes the foundation for navigating life's complexities with courage and tenacity.

2. **Redefining Success Beyond Conventions:** The Option B Revolution challenges conventional notions of success that are often tied to external

achievements and societal expectations. Success is redefined as a multifaceted concept that encompasses personal growth, well-being, adaptability, meaningful connections, and the pursuit of purpose. This shift acknowledges the diversity of paths towards fulfillment and encourages individuals to define success on their own terms.

3. **Embracing Alternatives and Possibilities:** Central to the Option B mindset is the idea of embracing alternatives and possibilities. When faced with unexpected twists in life, individuals are encouraged to see these challenges not as dead ends but as opportunities for growth and positive change. This perspective fosters creativity, innovation, and a proactive approach to navigating uncertainties.

4. **Building a Supportive Network:** The importance of building a strong support network is highlighted as a key takeaway. Meaningful connections with friends, family, mentors, and communities serve as a crucial foundation for emotional well-being and resilience. This support network provides empathy, understanding, and practical assistance,

creating a safety net during challenging times.

5. **Personal Growth as a Continuous Journey:** The Option B Revolution emphasizes that personal growth is a continuous journey rather than a destination. Challenges are viewed as opportunities for self-discovery, learning, and the development of untapped strengths. This perspective encourages individuals to approach life with curiosity, open-mindedness, and a commitment to ongoing self-improvement.

6. **Mindfulness and Reflection:** Mindfulness and reflection are integrated into the Option B Revolution as tools for self-awareness and intentional living. By practicing mindfulness, individuals create moments of stillness to observe their thoughts and emotions without judgment. This self-awareness enhances the ability to respond thoughtfully to challenges and fosters a deeper understanding of personal values.

7. **Finding Purpose in Adversity:** The Option B Revolution encourages individuals to find purpose in the midst of adversity. Rather than being defined by challenges, individuals are empowered to

align their actions with a sense of purpose, contributing to a greater good and making a positive impact on the world. Purpose becomes a guiding force that transcends individual difficulties.

8. **Creativity and Innovation in Problem-Solving:** The concept of embracing alternatives extends to problem-solving through creativity and innovation. Instead of being constrained by fixed perspectives, individuals are encouraged to explore alternative viewpoints, think outside traditional boundaries, and find innovative solutions to challenges. This adaptive approach contributes to a more resilient and solution-focused mindset.

9. **Balancing Ambition with Self-Care:** A key principle of the Option B Revolution is the recognition of the importance of balance between ambition and self-care. Pursuing ambitious goals is valued, but not at the expense of well-being. Balancing the drive for success with self-care practices ensures a sustainable approach to challenges, fostering long-term resilience and fulfillment.

10. **Expressing Gratitude Regularly:** The practice of expressing gratitude regularly is integrated into the Option B mindset.

Gratitude becomes a tool for cultivating a positive mindset, acknowledging the positive aspects of life, and fostering resilience. Regular expressions of gratitude contribute to a more optimistic and appreciative outlook.

11. **Inspiring and Supporting Others:** The Option B Revolution emphasizes the interconnectedness of individuals and encourages a culture of mutual support. By inspiring and supporting others on their journeys, individuals contribute to a positive and collaborative community. This reciprocal support creates a ripple effect, reinforcing the collective strength derived from shared experiences.

In conclusion, the Option B Revolution encapsulates a holistic and transformative approach to navigating life's challenges. It encourages individuals to cultivate resilience, redefine success on their own terms, embrace alternatives and possibilities, build a supportive network, view personal growth as a continuous journey, practice mindfulness and reflection, find purpose in adversity, foster creativity and innovation, balance ambition with self-care, express gratitude regularly, and inspire and support others. By internalizing these key principles and takeaways, individuals can embark on a journey of personal empowerment, growth, and resilience in the face of life's unexpected twists. The Option B Revolution becomes a guiding philosophy that empowers individuals to thrive amidst the complexities of life, fostering a positive and adaptive mindset for the challenges that lie ahead.

Redefine success on their terms and embrace the transformative power of life's Challenges

Encouraging to redefine success on their terms and embrace the transformative power of life's challenges is an invitation to embark on a journey of self-discovery, resilience, and purposeful living. It calls for a departure from traditional notions of success that are often externally defined, urging individuals to look inward and shape their own narratives of fulfillment.

Redefining Success on Your Terms:

The call to redefine success is an empowering proposition, urging readers to break free from societal expectations and predetermined benchmarks. It encourages introspection, asking individuals to identify what truly matters to them, beyond conventional measures of achievement. Success, in this context, becomes a personalized concept, intricately tied to one's values, passions, and individual aspirations. Readers are invited to view success not as a static destination but as a dynamic, evolving journey that aligns with their unique life paths.

Embracing the Transformative Power of Challenges:

Life's challenges are positioned as catalysts for transformation rather than impediments to success. Readers are encouraged to shift their perspective, viewing challenges not as setbacks but as opportunities for growth, learning, and self-discovery. The transformative power of challenges lies in their ability to shape character, deepen resilience, and unveil untapped strengths. By embracing challenges, individuals can navigate the complexities of life with a sense of purpose and adaptability, transcending adversities with newfound wisdom and strength.

Navigating the Unexpected Twists:

The encouragement to embrace life's unexpected twists is a recognition that the journey is inherently unpredictable. Rather than resisting change or fearing uncertainties, readers are invited to approach twists and turns with curiosity and openness. These unexpected moments become pivotal junctures for reevaluating priorities, adapting to new circumstances, and discovering alternative paths to success. Navigating the unexpected becomes a skill, a testament to one's ability to thrive in dynamic and ever-changing landscapes.

Cultivating Resilience in the Face of Adversity:

Resilience takes center stage as a key attribute in the journey of redefining success. Readers are prompted to cultivate resilience—a dynamic quality that enables them to bounce back from setbacks and continue forward with newfound strength. Adversity becomes a teacher, offering lessons in perseverance, self-discovery, and the art of turning challenges into stepping stones. The call to cultivate resilience is an acknowledgment that setbacks are not roadblocks but opportunities for personal and transformative growth.

Fostering a Positive Mindset:

Encouraging readers to redefine success and embrace life's challenges is inherently tied to fostering a positive mindset. It involves consciously choosing optimism over defeat, seeing possibilities in difficulties, and maintaining an attitude of gratitude. The transformative journey is paved with moments of self-reflection, where individuals consciously choose to focus on what they can control, rather than dwelling on what they cannot. A positive mindset becomes a powerful tool for navigating challenges and reshaping the narrative of success.

Discovering Purpose Amidst Adversity:

Amidst life's challenges, readers are urged to seek and discover their sense of purpose. Purpose becomes a guiding force that transcends external circumstances, providing individuals with a meaningful anchor in turbulent times. The transformative power lies in aligning actions with a deeper sense of purpose, turning challenges into opportunities to contribute positively to the world. Readers are invited to ask themselves what brings meaning to their lives and how they can infuse purpose into their journey of redefining success.

Empowering Personal Growth:

The call to redefine success and embrace life's challenges is, fundamentally, a call to embrace personal growth as an ongoing and transformative process. Growth is not confined to achievements or milestones but extends to the continuous evolution of one's character, skills, and perspectives. Each challenge becomes a stepping stone, propelling individuals forward on a journey of self-improvement, resilience, and adaptability. Personal growth becomes both the means and the end in the pursuit of redefined success.

In conclusion, encouraging readers to redefine success on their terms and embrace the transformative power of life's challenges is an invitation to embark on a journey of self-empowerment and purposeful living. It calls for a departure from societal expectations, urging individuals to view challenges not as stumbling blocks but as opportunities for growth and self-discovery. The transformative power lies in the intentional embrace of resilience, positive mindset, purpose, and ongoing personal growth. Through this journey, individuals can shape their own narratives of success, navigating the complexities of life with courage, adaptability, and a profound sense of purpose.

Ongoing Journey of growth and resilience in the face of life's uncertainties

As we reflect on the ongoing journey of growth and resilience in the face of life's uncertainties, it becomes evident that this transformative odyssey is not a destination but a perpetual evolution. Life, by its very nature, is a series of twists and turns, and the journey of growth and resilience is a continuous response to these dynamic challenges. In these concluding thoughts, we delve into the profound aspects of this journey, acknowledging its nuances and the enduring spirit required to navigate its complexities.

Embracing the Unpredictable:

The ongoing journey of growth and resilience is a testament to the ability to embrace the unpredictable nature of life. Uncertainties are not obstacles but rather opportunities for adaptation and innovation. By embracing the unpredictable, individuals open themselves to a world of possibilities, where each unforeseen event becomes a canvas for personal and collective growth. The journey is a celebration of the resilience that emerges when faced with the unknown, a testament to the capacity to thrive amidst the ebb and flow of life.

Learning from Setbacks:

Setbacks, rather than being seen as defeats, are integral to the ongoing journey of growth and resilience. Each setback offers a unique classroom for learning—the kind of education that cannot be gained in times of smooth sailing. Every stumble becomes a source of valuable insight, propelling individuals forward with a wealth of experience and newfound wisdom. The journey is a commitment to turning setbacks into stepping stones, transforming adversity into a catalyst for personal and collective advancement.

Adapting to Change:

Central to the ongoing journey is the art of adapting to change. Life's uncertainties often manifest as changes that require flexibility and openness. Resilience, in this context, is not just about bouncing back but about adapting and evolving in response to the evolving landscape. The ongoing journey encourages individuals to cultivate an agile mindset—one that can navigate the ever-shifting terrain with grace and a willingness to embrace the new.

Nurturing Inner Strength:

The journey of growth and resilience is a constant nurturing of inner strength. It requires a deep connection with one's inner reservoir of courage, determination, and self-belief. This inner strength becomes the bedrock upon which individuals stand when faced with life's uncertainties. It is a wellspring of resilience that, when tapped into, provides the fortitude needed to weather storms and emerge stronger on the other side.

Celebrating Small Victories:

Amidst the grand narrative of growth and resilience, the journey also involves celebrating the small victories along the way. Life is a collection of moments, and recognizing and reveling in the small triumphs contributes to a positive and empowered mindset. Whether overcoming a minor challenge or achieving a personal goal, these victories serve as milestones, markers of progress on the ongoing journey. The celebration of small victories is a practice in gratitude and a reminder that growth is a cumulative process.

Connecting with Others:

An integral facet of the ongoing journey is the recognition of the power of connection. Growth and resilience are not solitary endeavors; they thrive in the fertile soil of supportive relationships. The journey involves connecting with others—sharing experiences, offering support, and drawing strength from the collective resilience of a community. The bonds forged in the face of life's uncertainties become a source of inspiration, encouragement, and shared wisdom.

Staying Open to Possibilities:

The ongoing journey is a commitment to staying open to possibilities. It involves maintaining a curious and open-minded perspective that allows individuals to see opportunities even in the midst of challenges. By staying open, individuals invite innovation, creativity, and alternative solutions into their lives. This openness becomes a guiding principle, shaping the ongoing narrative of growth and resilience with a sense of optimism and anticipation.

Honoring the Process:

In these final thoughts, it is crucial to honor the process of growth and resilience. The journey is not about reaching a final destination but about embracing the continuous cycle of self-discovery and adaptation. Each phase of the process contributes to the overall tapestry of personal development. By honoring the process, individuals cultivate a deep sense of self-compassion and acceptance—a recognition that the journey itself is a profound achievement.

The Ever-Evolving Tapestry:

In conclusion, the ongoing journey of growth and resilience is an ever-evolving tapestry woven with the threads of adaptability, learning, connection, and inner strength. It is a celebration of the human spirit's capacity to not only endure but to flourish in the face of life's uncertainties. As individuals navigate the uncharted waters of their unique journeys, they become architects of their own narratives, shaping stories of triumph, resilience, and continual growth. The journey is an invitation to savor each step, learn from every twist, and embrace the beauty of becoming, for it is in the ongoing journey that the true essence of growth and resilience unfolds.